THE BIG PICTURE

A COMIC STRIP COLLECTION BY LENNIE PETERSON

Hope you
Loon of Do..
Comic strips
All the Best

**Andrews McMeel
Publishing**

Kansas City

Len Peterson
12/99

www.andrewsmcmeel.com

99 00 01 02 03 BAH 10 9 8 7 6 5 4 3 2 1

ISBN: 0-8362-7846-1

Library of Congress Catalog Card Number: 98-88675

INTRODUCTION

Here it is. Four years of my life and three hundred comic strips. All the highs and lows of Life and the adventure of trying to move from the world of "starving artist/musician" to the world of "Internationally Renowned Artist/Musician/Spiritual Leader/Sex Symbol/Zillionaire."

When I first left my teaching position at the Berklee College of Music, I sent several comic strip proposals to all of the major newspaper syndicates. For the most part, my proposals were run-of-the-mill cutesy comic strip premises with predictable sit-com punchlines or fuzzy-talking animals. Admittedly, I was trying to second-guess what the syndicates (and the "public") wanted. A "formula" that would make me tons of dough.

Stamping "CHEESEBALL SELLOUT" on my forehead would have achieved the same end. The reaction from most of the syndicates was pretty much, "Please stop sending us your run-of-the-mill cutesy comic strip premises with predictable sit-com punchlines and fuzzy-talking animals." I've gotten enough rejection letters over the years to wallpaper Gary Larson's mansion.

But a couple of syndicates did eventually write back telling me they liked my drawings.

Then it came: A personal note from Jay Kennedy at King Features Syndicate saying, "Lennie, I like your style but you should write more of what you KNOW." I took his words literally, and began writing about the subject I know best: me.

I offered my new concept to *Worcester Magazine* and they were the first to publish it on a weekly basis. "The Big Picture" then won *Editorial Humor Magazine's* 1995 nationwide Best Comic Strip contest and was noticed by Lee Salem at Universal Press Syndicate. UPS has never been afraid to take a risk on something they believe in. And an autobiographical comic strip about a bald, big-lipped fortiesh, divorced, workaholic, cat-owning, sex-crazed vegetarian/trombonist/cartoonist/ex-teacher from Worcester, Massachusetts, being a HUGE risk, I figured it was a match made in heaven.

Very long pain-in-the-ass-story-of-soul-searching-and-solving-some-of-Life's-mysteries made short, it is a match and here's a book of my comic strips thanks to Andrews McMeel.

Through better and worse, eighty percent of my comic strip is one hundred percent reality. The other twenty percent is reality with a little twist for a half-decent punchline. Any resemblance to persons living or dead are completely intentional (even if the cartoon doesn't exactly resemble them) except where I've been threatened with lawsuits.

Hope you enjoy it.

May you someday realize that your life is a comic strip too and through better and worse, it's all a part of YOUR story. And may you enjoy the ride . . .

This book is dedicated to the Soul, Spirit, and Inspiration of my mother, Shirley Peterson

 Thanks to All of the Following FoR their **UNCONDITIONAL** Love And SuppoRT

| dAd | MiLLie | MoM | CHRISTiNE |  BRUCE | todd | MELiNDA | MARK | keViN | JACKie |

| LOUiSE | PATRiK | Mathieu | MAX | SAMMie |  Clutch GRABWELL |  ESpeciAlly MARK / MY HiGHER SELF | GiNGER who gets MORE MAiL thaN I do |

| JENN | LiZ | BReNDA My LANDLORD | WORCESTER MAGAZiNE | WALTER CROCKEtt | My heART (ouch) | My StoMaCH / My LiVER | Lee SALEM FoR his ViSiON |

| WHOeVER discoVeReD COFFEE | THE WORCESTER PHOENiX | ESpeciAlly MELiSSA | SAM AdAms | DUNKiN' DONUTS | THE LANCASTER TiMES / ESpeciAlly PAUL | shelly | |

| SUSAN HeRR | JoLeNe 1 |  JoLeNe 2 | My tROMBONE | DORothy O'BRieN WHATeVeR SHe LooKs Like | ANDREWS McMEEL PUBL. | BONNIE |

|  PABLO PiCASSO FOR PROViNG EVeRything |  MiLLiONS OF 'EM! All the FANS OF My COMiC STRiP | ? ANyONE I'M FoRGeTTiNG who diDN't SAy this couLDN't Be doNE |  DAWN FoR BeiNG theRe WHeN I discoVeReD "It" |

| YOUR FACE HERE (FiND ME! I'll dRAW it!) YOU, FOR BUYiNG My Book |  AND LAST BUT NOT LEAST, the UNiVeRSe FoR its MAGNETiC GRiD AND the LAW OF AttRAction |

I'VE BEEN PLAYING the tROMBONE PROFESSIONALLY FOR OVER twenty YEARS

I REMEMBER AS A Little kid SEEING the BEATLES ON Ed SULLIVAN. It WAS then and there I WANTED to GROW up to BE A Rich And FAMOUS ROCK STAR SO I took UP AN INSTRUMENT

NeAto!

(I WAS A GOOFY KID)

JUST Yesterday I REALIZED I'VE dEVoted MY ENTIRE LIFE to MUSIC BUt I'M **STILL** Not Rich And FAMOUS Yet

BILL $

EVICTION OVERDUE PAY NOW! NOTICE

Then it Suddenly OCCURRED tO ME

THE BEATLES NEVER EVEN **HAd** A tROMBONE PLAYER

Oops

with Apologies to Aaron Copeland

THE Big PICTURE

by Lennie "How Come Nobody Likes Me?" Peterson

HAPPY THANKSGIVING!

I WENT TO MY FRIEND'S HOUSE LAST YEAR TO JOIN HER FAMILY FOR THANKSGIVING DINNER.

IT WAS HELL.

TURKEY, ERNIE?

UM.. IT'S "LENNIE" AND NO THANKS. I'VE BEEN A VEGETARIAN FOR TWENTY YEARS

A WHAT?!

C'MON... HAVE A LITTLE MEAT- IT WON'T KILL YOU

WHAT ARE YOU, A GIRLY-MAN?

THAT'S WHY YOU'RE SICK ALL THE TIME, ERNIE

PROBABLY A BUDDHIST. SISSY COMMIE FREAK

HAM? HOW 'BOUT HAM?

NEXT YEAR I THINK I'LL JUST STAY HOME AND GIVE THANKS MY CAT CAN'T TALK

WHAT ARE YOU, A GIRLY-MAN?

Lennie Peterson

8

It's important to spend New Year's Eve with your significant other

The partner that's been with you through thick and thin

For better or worse in good times and bad with complete and unconditional love

And, as always, I'll be kissing mine at midnight

to the guy at Shaw's supermarket this morning— you were wearing a red coat and a Nike cap... you said—

Hey!...this is a ten item lane...you have eleven items there!

You

Number one, it was eleven items because I had a "two for one" package of Rice-A-Roni...Two, I'm exhausted from working eighteen stoopid hours a stoopid day so I didn't see the stoopid "ten items only" sign... Three, my **divorce** from Louise just got finalized this morning and I'm depressed and the **LAST** friggin' thing I feel like doing is answering to a friggin' "checkout line police" wanna-be who can't mind his own business... and four,→

BITE ME

thank you

THE BIG PICTURE

by Lennie "Cartoonist/Artist/Musician/Sex Symbol/Spiritual Leader/Hero to Zillions" Peterson

WHOA! CHECK **HER** OUT! SHE'S AN **ELEVEN!**

NAH... I DON'T LIKE HER **NOSE**

HER **NOSE?**

TOO "CUTE"... TOO "BARBIE"... I'M INTO NOSES WITH **CHARACTER**

ANYONE I'VE **EVER** BEEN ATTRACTED TO HAS HAD A NOSE THAT MADE A **STATEMENT**

NOW **THAT'S** SEXY =sigh=

THERE ARE "LEG-MEN," "BUTT-MEN" AND "BREAST-MEN"

I HAVE TO BE CURSED WITH "NOSE-MAN"

GUITAR FUN FACTS

UNBEKNOWNST TO MOST MUSICOLOGISTS, **JIMI HENDRIX** STARTED PLAYING GUITAR ONLY AFTER HE DISCOVERED THAT HIS TROMBONE WOULDN'T IGNITE

LAST YEAR I spent countless HOURS IN MY CAR travelling TO MY GIGS

SOMETIMES I WONDER IF this CONSTANT QUEST FOR FAME AND FORTUNE IS WORTH ALL the PERSONAL AND EMOTIONAL SACRIFICE

BUT HERE'S WHAT I WONDER MOST OF ALL:

WHERE'S the NEAREST "DUNKIN' DONUTS"?

DUE to LAST NIGHT'S SNOW, ALL CLASSES IN every school EVERYWHERE ARE CANCELLED FOREVER

MY CAT HAS APPEARED IN this COMIC STRIP ONLY FIVE times IN THE LAST YEAR

BUT SHE GETS **Alot** MORE MAIL THAN I DO

SO, IN THE INTEREST OF FREE ENTERPRISE (AND MY WALLET), the NAME OF this STRIP will BE CHANGED to "GINGER"

It will FEATURE ONLY MY CAT AND HER WACKY ADVENTURES

NOW IF I could JUST GET HER to **DO** SOMETHING

the BiG PiCTURE

by Lennie "NOW A MEMBER OF THE FORTUNE 950,000,000" PETERSON

the following is A true story—
I swear on my
Brand New Sharpies
And my
Brand New
Brush!

YEE-HA!!

LAST week I tried to pay my overdue car insurance in Person

I'M SORRY, SIR BUT YOU HAVE TO **MAIL** YOUR PAYMENT—

Next, Please!

I CAN WRITE A check!

SIR...YOU HAVE TO **MAIL** YOUR PAYMENT

But if I **MAIL** it, then it'll be too late And my insurance will be **CANCELLED**

I'M SORRY, SIR... **NEXT, PLEASE**

I took A **MENTAL** Fit

LISTEN, YOU BLUE HAIRED OLD BAG - IF YOU don't take my money I'M GONNA SHOVE this BILL Right up your **BiG GOOFY NOSE!!**

Well... Actually Not that much OF A mental Fit... it WAS more Like this—

Jeez

Next

I PLAY IN A BAND CALLED "Clutch GRABWELL"

THE leader of the BAND, MARK, ACTUALLY HAD THE NERVE to ASK ME to SNEAK A PROMOTION FOR Next week's gig INTO this comic strip!

IMAGINE HIM ASKING ME to Plug OUR SHOW AT the PLANTATION CLUB IN WORCESTER, MA. Next FRIDAY Night JANUARY 24 STARTING AT 10 P.M.

He EVEN WANTED me to mention that You CAN ORDER OUR New C.d. AT Clutch GRABWell P.O. Box 415 Hull, MA. 02045... MARK EVEN OFFERED to PAY me FOR THE Plug!

THE GALL... DOES HE ACTUALLY think I CAN BE Bought?!

COFFEE?

BREAK FAST

I CALLED MY EDitor AT WORCESTER MAGAZINE YESTERDAY

Hi...WALTER CROCKETT PLEASE

Hi, WALTER? I'M JUST CALLING to MAKE SURE YOU RECEIVED MY CARTOON FOR THIS WEEK

YA, It's HERE

AND...UM...ALSO... UM...did YOU GET MY NOTE ABOUT... UM...MAYBE GIVING ME A RAISE IN PAY?

OH YA! thanks!

NOW that's A good LAUGH!

THE BIG PICTURE presents ILLUSIONARY ART!

The Latest Craze Sweeping the Country!!

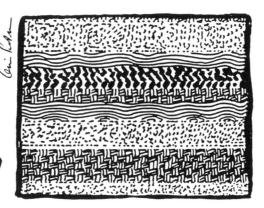

INSTRUCTIONS
1. Hold the IMAGE CLOSE to your FACE
2. Slowly move the PAGE AWAY while STARING AT THE IMAGE
3. Keep STARING AND WAIT FOR A PICTURE TO APPEAR
4. REALIZE YOU HAVE WAY TOO MUCH TIME ON YOUR HANDS
5. Get A LIFE

THIS EPISODE: LENNIE GROWS A BEARD!

COMING SOON: LENNIE SHAVES

There are certain advantages to being a cartoon character

1 Like those little kids from the "Family Circus," I'll never have to grow old

This is Cool

In **REAL** life we'd be **Eighty** and sitting in a nursing home!

2 Sometimes people recognize me on the street

Hey! You look just like your drawings of yourself!!

Gee, thanks... — I think

3 Someday I'll get to be a suction cup doll

4 I'm not wearing any pants

Beavis, Dolly, Binky, Billy and Garfield appear courtesy of somebody, somewhere.

17

The Big Picture

BY LENNIE "CREAM, ONE SUGAR" PETERSON

I **LOVE** coffee... IN ANY WAY, SHAPE OR FORM*

Hot Coffee →
iced Coffee →
Coffee Cake →

Coffee to go →
Coffee ice Cream →

Coffee to stay →
Even decaf PROBABLY HAS A PURPOSE

* 'CEPT COFFEE CANDY... YUCK.

THANKS TO THE MIRACLES OF MODERN TECHNOLOGY AND MY AUTOMATIC COFFEE POT TIMER, I WAKE UP TO A FRESHLY BREWED CUP O' JOE EACH AND EVERY A.M.

GURGLE GURGLE

YES!

I WISH **EVERYTHING** could smell and taste like coffee*

BREATH MINTS

 JAVAMINT

BEER

PERFUME

 AIR FRESH-ENER

GREEN BEANS →

* 'cept CANDY... yuck.

NUCLEAR WASTE →

I AVERAGE SEVEN to ten CUPS A dAy
(HOW 'BOUT YOU?) Huh?

I MEAN I **REALLY** LOVE COFFEE

COFFEE

I ASKED MY FRIEND LIZ IF SHE thinks She'll Get MARRIED SomeDAY

I GUESS SO... **I'd** LiKe A GUY AROUNd the HOUSE to do All the Stoopid GUY Stuff — y'KNOW, LiKe Fix the CAR, do the PLUMBING... **GUY** Stuff

BUt WHAT ABOUt COMPANIONSHIP ANd PASSION? FRieNdship ANd **LOVE?**

I'd LiKe A GUY AROUNd the HOUSE to do the Stoopid GUY Stuff

FORGet the J.F.K. ASSASiNATION... FORGet U.F.O.s FORGet Red M and Ms... **THESE ARE the REAL CONSPIRACIES** →

① Book Bindings

WHY ARE they PRINTed LiKe **this?** →

Why CAN't they Be PRINTed LiKe **this?**... OR **Stacked** LiKe this → THIS SIDE UP ↑

Huh?? **Hello??**

② CABLE t.v. Listings

See WHAT time the movie is ON... I think it's ON CBS which is CABLE FOURTEEN ON T.B.T. which is the SAME AS CHANNEL NINE

③ WISE-ASS HAiRdRessers

THERE'S NO **WAY** I CAN CHARGe You Full PRICE FOR this

21

REGISTRY OF MOTOR VEHICLES →

SNACKS

SODA

CAMPING EQUIPMENT

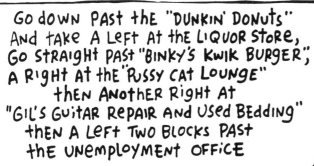

GO DOWN PAST THE "DUNKIN' DONUTS"
AND TAKE A LEFT AT THE LIQUOR STORE,
GO STRAIGHT PAST "BINKY'S KWIK BURGER",
A RIGHT AT THE "PUSSY CAT LOUNGE"
THEN ANOTHER RIGHT AT
"GIL'S GUITAR REPAIR AND USED BEDDING"
THEN A LEFT TWO BLOCKS PAST
THE UNEMPLOYMENT OFFICE

IS THAT "DUNKIN' DONUTS" A DRIVE-THRU?

MUSICIANS' DIRECTIONS

I think I WAS the ONLY CARTOONIST At the SMALL BUSINESS Administration tAx SeminAr

SO, REMEMBER, FORM S.T.S.Q-4 CAN Be USED FOR Item 32 depending ON YOUR C.M.I. STATUS And YOUR Fiduciary Withholding Exemption

ANY QUESTIONS?

OH! I HAVE ONE! CAN I GEt A Refund FOR All the MONEY I SPENT ON "FRISKIES" FOR MY CAT Ginger?

well, I dRAW HER **Alot**

the BIG PICTURE

by Lennie "No Line Between my Life and this Stoopid comic strip" Peterson

I'm really HORRIBLE at repairing things... like ANYthing... it's EMBARRASSING 'cause it's supposed to be a "GUY" thing

CAN you look at this for me? It's BROKE

SURE... WHAT is it?

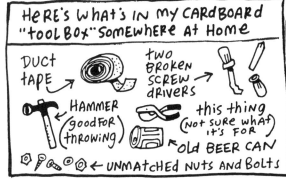

HERE'S WHAT'S IN MY CARDBOARD "tool BOX" SOMEWHERE AT HOME

DUCT TAPE →

two BROKEN SCREW DRIVERS →

HAMMER (good for throwing) →

this thing (not sure what it's for)

← OLD BEER CAN

← UNMATCHED NUTS AND BOLTS

And HERE ARE my THREE EASY steps to REPAIRING EVERYthing FROM SHOES to CARS!

Hey! You CAN Use 'em too!! (don't FORGET your hammer!) →

STEP ONE: SWEAR At it

Stop dripping you ☆ⓖ#⌗#〰☆☆ⓖ FAUCEt!!

Step two: IF SWEARING DOESN'T WORK USE LOTS OF duct tape

Step THREE: IF the duct tape doesn't WORK, sell it

HOUSE FOR SALE CHEAP AS IS (FAUCEt SUCKS)

I went to the store yesterday

Hey, wow! Nice to **see** you! You look **great**!

Hi!... Thanks!*

*Gee...she must be a fan of my band... maybe she saw me on t.v.... I think she likes me...kinda cute, too!

I'm Cindy... I'll be right back

Okay, Cindy... I'll be here!*

*She's probably taken by my irresistible charm and huge lips...probably in **love** with me

Hey, wow! Nice to **see** you! You look **great**!

Hi!... Thanks!

Hello, is this Bob's Exterminating? ...I think I've got a **problem** here

LENNIE PETERSON IS A MASS MURDERER!

COCKROACH RIGHTS

STOP THE GENOCIDE

This week The Big Picture Salutes :TEACHERS:

I remember... I was **one** of you... oh my **god** do I remember!

The students' quest for knowledge

And that adds up to sixty percent... any questions?

Ya... can I be excused? I gotta pee wicked bad

the pay check

Lemme see...gross minus fica, social security, insurance, taxes... **excellent!** Just enough left over to buy some prizes for the class treasure hunt!

the reward

Hey, Mr. Crowley... how come I got a "D" on my report?

It was a gift

SUSAN POWTER'S DAY OFF

THE BIG PICTURE

BY LENNIE "don't try this at home, I'm A PROFESSIONAL" PETERSON

LENNIE, WHY DO YOU DRAW HANDS WITH ONLY THREE FINGERS?

All the GREATS have done it, MATT

disney, kelly, WATTER-SON... **All** the greats!

It GIVES the CARTOON its OWN UNIQUE CHARACTER TRAIT... YOU SEE, the **HAND** IS the ULTIMATE tool OF HUMAN EXPRESSION AND the simplicity OF utilizing ONLY THREE FINGERS ALLOWS the ARTIST EXAGGERATED ARTICULATION!

YOU HAVE NO CLUE WHAT YOU'RE TALKING ABOUT, do YOU?

NO... I think MAYBE it SAVES INK

It's pretty cool how DOGS have no concept of their own size

...FOR INSTANCE, MY 110 POUND Retriever IS TERRIFIED OF MY FRIEND LISA'S Little terrier-

I WAS thinking... FOR LISA'S SAKE AND EVERY OTHER WOMAN That's EVER BEEN ABUSED BY A GUY...

It WOULD BE AN EVEN COOLER HUMAN TRAIT

AVOiding LAWSuits IN the NiNeties

←DON'T LiCK YOUR HANDS AFTER YOU touch this

← TRIPPiNG ON this could HURT

WARNING: Hot WATER MAY CAUSE YOU to SAY "OUCH, that's Hot"↴

Looking IN HERE Could BE SCARY ←

Don't drop YOUR COMB

CAUTION: Reading this Sign REPeatedly could CAUSE EYE FATigue

Attention: USING iNSUFFICIENT Amounts OF toilet PAPER MAY CAUSE HYGiENE Complications →

WARNING: Flushing causes drowning IN LABRATORY GoldFish→

don't FORGET YOUR PANTS

It WAS 1978 I had Joined A LOCAL ROCK BAND AND WAS Feeling PRETTY FULL OF MYSELF

Me with HAiR·1978

The MAGiC MOMENT ARRiVED ONE SUNNY DAY iN kelly SQUARE, WORCESTER

BEEP   Beep

GO- IF YOU FEEL LIKE IT →

FOR the FIRST TIME, SOMEONE RECOGNIZED ME!

Hey! AREN'T YOU IN A BAND?

Why, YES, I AM!

It WAS MY FIRST taste OF Celebrity StatuS

YOU GUYS SUCK!

27

Panel 1: MY FRIEND **LIKES** YOU, LENNIE... AND SHE'S **BEAUTIFUL**... WHY DON'T YOU WANT TO GO OUT WITH HER?

'CAUSE I'VE **SEEN** THE GUYS SHE DATES... BUFFED UP, SPORTS-ADDICTED, MACHO MORONS WHO TREAT HER LIKE **CRAP**... PLUS SHE'S GOT **NO** SENSE OF HUMOR AND THE I.Q. OF A **TOASTER**... LIKE, **BRAIN**-LESS

Panel 2: Oh.. AND I SUPPOSE **YOU'RE** GOD'S GIFT TO WOMEN? A DIVORCED, BROKE, WORKAHOLIC ARTIST/MUSICIAN **PSYCHO**

Panel 3: SEE WHAT I MEAN? I WOULD **NEVER** DATE ANYONE STOOPID ENOUGH TO GO OUT WITH SOMEONE LIKE ME

Panel 4: DON'T FORGET TO VOTE THIS TUESDAY

Panel 5: ITEM #66A IS **VERY** IMPORTANT

Panel 6: **PLEASE** VOTE "YES"

Panel 7: #66A - All citizens are automatically prohibited to vote for any political candidate who stands on a street corner with a giant goofy sign smiling and waving at passing cars like a big silly DORK

Panel 8: MIKE AND I WENT OUT FOR A DRINK LAST NIGHT — HI! I'M LENNIE! CARE TO JOIN US FOR A DRINK?

Panel 9: YA, RIGHT

Panel 10: OBVIOUSLY TWO **MORE** HELPLESS CREATURES THREATENED BY YOUR INTIMIDATING CELEBRITY STATUS UNABLE TO CONTEND WITH THE OVERWHELMING GLOW OF YOUR SEXUAL MAGNETISM

The Big Picture

by Lennie "No Wonder I can't get Syndicated" Peterson

I get upset every single morning

INCREDIBLE

Comics

UH-OH

Most of the comics **SUCK**... especially this one about the Big Stoopid **dog**...every day it's the same thing...the Big Stoopid dog is placed in some UNFUNNY **HUMAN** setting but because it's a Big Stoopid **DOG**, it's supposed to be **FUNNY**

Today the Big Stoopid dog was on a Riding **LAWN MOWER!!**... what the Hell is **FUNNY** about that?...that cartoonist makes like a **Zillion** dollars a **day** "creating" that **CRAP!!**

This is an outrageous **BILKING** of the **AMERICAN PUBLIC!!**

DAMN

Wish **I** thought of that

29

"ALEXA" LEARNS to BE MORE SPECIFIC WHEN TAKING OUT A PERSONAL AD IN the LOCAl ALTERNATIVE

Hi, I'm CALLING ABOUT YOUR Ad SEEKING A t.v. Did You WANT A PORTABLE OR A CONSOLE?

HEY! LOOK!! It's LAst week's Strip ExplAiNED!

(BECAUSE WE HERE AT "the Big Picture" WANT you to Get it !! ...WE CARE!!)

SEE, this GUY is dRESSED Up LiKE A WOMAN- HE'S A tRANSVEStiTE - ABBREViATED AS "T.V."...SO, ANYWAY, HIS NAME is "ALEXA" AND HE'S getting A CALL FROM AN Ad HE PLACED, BUT the CALLER thinks it's AN Ad FOR A tELEViSion AND...oh, FORGEt it.

title OF Strip →

MY NAME - LOOMING LARGER THAN LIFE itSELF (I LiVE FOR this)

NOW PLEASE Stop CALLING ME - THANK YOU

THE BIG PICTURE by Lennie Peterson

"ALEXA" LEARNS to BE MORE SPECIFIC WHEN TAKING OUT A PERSONAL AD IN the LOCAl ALTERNATIVE

(AS iN ALTERNATIVE NEWSPAPER)

Hi, I'm CALLING ABOUT YOUR Ad SEEKING A t.v. Did You WANT A PORTABLE OR A CONSOLE?

LAMP (this is NOT A tele-Vi-Sion) PHONE

'ALEXA' ↑

SEE? This is A GUY (MUSTACHE, SIDEBURNS, STUBBLE, FALLiNG FALSIES) (COME to think OF it, it LOOKS LiKE A GiRL I dAtED iN HighSchool)

THIS IS **NOT** A SLAM AGAINST idiots GUYS WHO SECRETLY CROSS-DRESS...SOME OF MY BEST FRiENDS CROSS dRESS (YOU KNOW who you ARE, you CREEPS)

This week, WE dig iNTO the MOUNDS OF FAN MAiL RECEIVED HERE At "the Big Picture"

WHOA! A Letter!

This one's FROM MARiA IN Seattle

Dear Lennie, Who's that guy with the beard and glasses that's always in your comic strip? Are we supposed to know him? Thanks, MARiA

P.S. I LOVE YOU!!! *

* I MAdE that PART up

DEAR MARiA-That's MY FRiEND, Mike. HE'S iN A BAND with ME. HE'S A GREAT SAX PLAYER AND ONE OF MY FAVORiTE PEOPLE. HiS APPEARANCES HERE ARE MY PERSONAL tRibUTE TO HiS FiNE CHARACTER

ACTUALLY the truth is...

He's Just REALLY EASY to dRAW

God's Eighth day

Happy Holidays!

UNIVERSAL REPAIR

OPEN

PLANETS OUR SPECIALTY

HAPPY NEW YEAR

FROM ALL OF US AT "THE BIG PICTURE"

I hope you all had a peaceful and joyous holiday

And I hope your band didn't get stiffed **500** bucks by a **LOSER** club owner on New Year's Eve

And I hope when you stick your trombone up his nose you can get your trombone back again

So you can **REINSERT** it **Sideways**

And I hope you all have a peaceful and joyous New Year

THE BIG PICTURE

by Lennie "have a nice friggin' day" Peterson

AS USUAL, I WAS MINDING MY OWN BUSINESS ON A SET BREAK

Glug Glug

Hi!... Lennie, right?

YA, HI *

* UH OH

Like, YOU GUYS SOUND WICKED AWESOME

thanks

* "wicked AWESOME"? WHO HAVE YOU BEEN HANGIN' OUT WITH, BART SIMPSON?

I SEEN YOU GUYS BEFORE... YOU'RE PISSA

Uh Huh *

* AND WHERE'D YOU GET those clothes, the Jed Clampett memorial dumpster fire sale?

AND YOUR SOLO WAS COOL, dood

Thanks... Hey, maybe I'll talk to you later, okay?

* WE'LL GO BACK to YOUR PLACE AND PLAY "MEAN OLD BALD VEGETARIAN MUSICIAN/ARTIST DUNGEON MASTER"

She loves me

Jeez... what a JERK

I USED to PLAY WEDDINGS WITH the JERRY SEECO BAND. It WAS COOL BECAUSE JERRY NEVER did ANYTHING HE didn't **WANT** TO DO

ONCE, I heard A BRIDE REQUEST A SONG

CAN YOU PLAY "THE CHICKEN dANCE"?

JERRY SAID:

NO

SHE ASKED WHY NOT

Why NOT?

JERRY ACTUALLY SAID THIS—

'CAUSE THAT SONG **SUCKS**

MAN, I tell YA... It SCARED THE **HELL** OUT OF ME... It HAPPENED RIGHT HERE WHILE I WAS EATING MY BURGER AND FRIES

YOU'RE KIDDING! THAT'S **AWFUL**

THE GUY CAME OVER, STUCK A GUN IN MY FACE AND STOLE MY **WALLET**

Jeez, I CAN'T BELIEVE it

A BURGER AND FRIES... HOW CAN YOU **EAT** THAT CRAP?

HERE IN THE CITY, WE HAVE A RITUAL AFTER A SNOW STORM

AFTER YOU SHOVEL YOUR CAR OUT

YOU RESERVE "YOUR" SHOVELED SPOT ON THE STREET BY PLACING AN OLD CHAIR OR SOMETHING IN THAT SPACE

MY NEIGHBOR, PAUL, GETS REALLY CARRIED AWAY

TIM NAERING IS A FAN OF THE BAND I'M IN. HE WAS AT OUR GIG LAST NIGHT

I'M NOT INTO SPORTS BUT I THOUGHT IT WOULD BE COOL TO MEET SOMEONE FAMOUS

Hi! I'M LENNIE... I DON'T FOLLOW BASKETBALL BUT I **do** HEAR YOU'RE A PRETTY GOOD QUARTERBACK FOR THE BRUINS!

HE WASN'T VERY FRIENDLY

I'VE GOT A **GIANT** BOTTOM LIP

Jeez... **LOOK** AT THAT thing

"TRACY" IS THIS **REALLY** CUTE WAITRESS I KNOW. SHE'S GOT A HUGE TOP LIP... EVEN BIGGER THAN HER **BOTTOM** LIP!!

I dig that

I'M GONNA ASK HER TO DUMP HER DOPEY BOYFRIEND AND HAVE MY BABY...

I NEED THE CASH

SEE!! "LIPS" LIVE AND IN THE FLESH!! THE WONDER BABY

ENTER

ADMISSION $5.00

He's ALL LIP!!

The Big Picture

BY LENNIE "WOMEN SWOON, MEN CHEER" PETERSON

...and the tattooed biker chick with the pierced tonque, leather mini skirt, and fishnet stockings reading the Pablo Picasso biography clenching a bullwhip and a bottle of Jack Daniels looked up from her vegetarian cheese burger in amazement...

"Oh my God!" she exclaimed. "You're a cartoonist AND a trombone player?!!"

"Where have you been?! I've been searching for you my entire LIFE!!"

And so they lived happily ever after as reclusive hermits obsessed with each other while ignoring the rest of the world and the stoopid people in it.

OKAY, UNCLE LENNIE...that's the SEVENTH time you've READ that ONE... NOW CAN YOU READ ME "THE THREE Little Pigs"?

JUST ONCE MORE

YOU'RE ASKING ME IF I'M **GAY**?!

SO, WHAT JERRY SEINFELD SAID IS **TRUE**? IF YOU'RE A MALE WHO'S THIN, NEAT, CREATIVE AND NOT INTO **FOOTBALL** PEOPLE ASSUME THAT YOU'RE **GAY**?

WELL, Y'KNOW, PLUS YOU'RE SENSITIVE AND NICE AND STUFF

OH YA? WELL, HOW'S **THIS**?!

GO PATS

I LOVE MY JOB

THIS AWARD TRULY IS A DREAM COME TRUE

AND I'D LIKE TO THANK YOU FOR BEING THERE THROUGH IT ALL... SILENT, BRAVE, SUPPORTIVE, UNQUESTIONING!

BUT I'D ESPECIALLY LIKE TO THANK MYSELF...

FOR CREATING THESE AWARDS

THE FIRST ANNUAL 37 YEAR OLD CARTOONIST/TROMBONIST VEGETARIAN BALD GUYS NAMED "LENNIE" AWARD

PRESENTING
A "BIG PICTURE"
PUBLIC SERVICE

THE ALL
NEW
LENNIE
PETERSON

2 STEP DIET PLAN!

JUST **LOOK** AT THESE RESULTS!

It's Quick too!

BEFORE AFTER

STEP ONE:
BECOME A MUSICIAN
Step two:
STARVE

It WAS NICE to MEET YOU, LENNIE

THANKS FOR inviting ME BACK to YOUR PLACE BUT I CAN'T...

I'm Allergic to CATS

How'd SHE KNOW I HAVE A **CAT**?

---

the Following IS TRUE— I SWEAR ON MY BOTTLE OF INDIA INK

A FEW YEARS BACK I WENT to MY doctor 'CAUSE I HAD SOME CHEST PAINS

do You do ANY HEAVY LIFTING?

NO, BUT I CARRY MY INSTRUMENT CASE ON MY SHOULDER ALL THE TIME

REALLY? WHAT INSTRUMENT do You PLAY?

TROMBONE

(this is AN ACTUAL QUOTE)

WHY?

37

THE BiG PiCTURE

by LENNIE "BeNeFits, ShmeNeFits" PeTeRSON

PeTeRSON · SCRAM

Hey... SECRETARIES DAY WAS LAST WEEK

YA...SO?

SO... WHERE'S MY GIFT? A **BONUS** MAYBE?

I'VE GOT YOUR BONUS, PAL

Right HERE

YOU ARE A **JERK** OF A BOSS

And **YOU** ARE A HORRIBLE SECRETARY

OH, YA? Well YOUR Stoopid Comic Strip **SUCKS**

It keeps **YOU** Fed, YOU BiG LiPPED **CUE BALL!**

HA! BARELY! WHY DON'T YOU SHUT UP OR I'll GO Find A **REAL JOB!**

WHEW

Self Employment CAN Be **ROUGH**

38

I HAVE MY MOM'S ARTISTIC TALENTS

MY DAD'S MUSICAL TALENTS

GRAMMY COLEMAN'S SENSE OF HUMOR

GRAMPY PETERSON'S WORK ETHIC AND DISCIPLINE

HAPPY MOTHER'S DAY

TO DO
1. WORK
2. WORK
3. WORK
4. WORK
5. WORK
6. WORK
WORK

...AND GINGER'S SHEDDING

DAMN

BAD HAIR DECADE

PAUL DELLA VALLE AND I HAVE A HUMOR BOOK COMING OUT

WELCOME TO YOUR MIDLIFE CRISIS!

IT'LL BE IN BOOKSTORES NATIONWIDE THIS SUMMER

$

WE'RE DOING A BOOK-SIGNING AT THE PLANT-ATION CLUB IN WORCESTER THIS FRIDAY STARTING AT 8 P.M. IT WILL GO ALL NIGHT

LIVE MUSIC WITH THE JOEYS!

BUFFET

BEER

BOOKS

MORE BEER

GET THERE EARLY... WHO KNOWS WHAT OUR SIGNATURES WILL LOOK LIKE BY MIDNIGHT

DRIVE THRU TELLER →

OVER DRAWN

EXIT

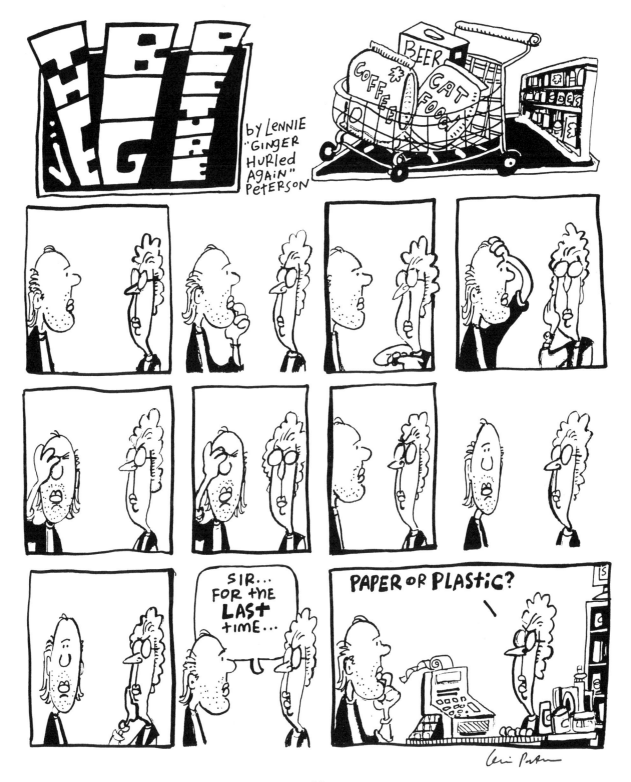

MUSICIAN FOOD GROUPS

MEAT AND POULTRY

FRUITS AND VEGETABLES

DAIRY

GRAINS AND CEREALS

YOU MAKE ME FEEL LIKE A TOTAL **idiot**

You're domineering, intimidating AND **UNAPPROACHABLE**

AND IF YOU think I'm GOING to Put up with it ANY LONGER...

...You're **CRAZY**

Oh, ya?

...well, YOU'RE the one who talks to your COMPUTER

THE BiG PicTuRe **PReSeNTS** "The **LoViNG HuSBaND**"!

(FiLe UNDeR "I" FOR "I think it's JUST A FIGURE OF SPEECH)

I OVERHEARD this AT the SUPERMARKET yesterday— WORD FOR WORD

Gee...it's **FREEZING** iN HeRe

Well I douBt **VERY** much that it's ActuALLy thirty two DeGrees

God, honey... **THiNK** FOR A CHANGE, will you?

WhAt A dORK

I'm doing lots of soul searching And I've made quite a few changes in my approach to life -

these days, I'm trying to live in the MOMENT -

And Follow My NATURE... y'know, Be SPONTANEOUS

Sometimes it really SUCKS

SLAP

ouch

FARTING, NO FARTING OR FIRST AVAILABLE?

THE BIG PICTURE

by LENNIE "Approved by SOME Reviewer Somewhere" PETERSON

PLAYING THE TROMBONE HAS its definite ADVANTAGES

I GET to MEET LOTS OF WOMEN

Hi! I'm KATHY! CAN YOU INTRODUCE US to the **DRUMMER**?

It's FUN LISTENING to People try to FIGURE Out what its CALLED

Hey! GREAT tRUMPET SOLO!.. ER... SAXOPHONE.. tUBA... WHATEVER... that **thing**

Thanks

I SAVE TONS OF MONEY ON LiP ENLARGiNG COLLAGEN INJECTIONS

TOUGH GiG?

There's A wide VARiety OF INTERESTING AND CHALLENGING GIGS AVAiLABLE

IF YOU EVER NEED to ACTUALLY EARN MONEY with it, A tROMBONE MAKES A GREAt LAMP

HONK

Stoopid thing...
YOU'RE SO
SLOW

Beep

CLICK
CLICK
CLICK

Oh, YA?
Wanna see
SLOW?

Huh?

That pencil,
that paper,
and your
BRAIN...

Now, THAT
would be
SLOW!

I used to
teach at
Berklee
College
of music.
I once
substituted
for my
friend,
Jerry
Seeco

... AND SO the "A" BECOMES
TENSION THIRTEEN AND All
of the NOTES COMBINED
BECOME AN "UPPER
STRUCTURE TRIAD"

ANY
QUES-
TIONS?

I HAVE A QUESTION

Yes?

WHEN IS MR. SEECO
COMING BACK?

YA...
MR. SEECO
IS **COOL**

YA

How long
HAVE YOU
HAD YOUR
CAT?

ABOUT
A YEAR...
WE HAVE
A DEAL
WORKED
OUT

ZZZ

A deal?
WHAT
kind of
deal?

ZZZ

I take care of her,
Feed her, GROOM her,
make her Life Better
than Ninety eight
percent of All the
People in the world...

And in
RETURN SHE
Allows ME
to **Live**
with her

LUCKY YOU,
CARTOON
BOY

45

MUZAK IN THE REALLY RITZY RESTAURANTS

I SHOULD PROBABLY NEVER JOIN AMERICA'S CORPORATE WORK FORCE

I SHOULD PROBABLY NEVER JOIN AMERICA'S CORPORATE WORK FORCE

I SHOULD PROBABLY NEVER JOIN AMERICA'S CORPORATE WORK FORCE

the big picture

by LENNIE "PERHAPS you'd LiKE to dRAW YOUR LittLE CARTOONS DOWN At tHE PRiNCiPAL'S OFFICE, LEONARD "PETERSON

FOR A CARTOONIST, tHE ROAd to **GARFIELD** FAME ANd FORTUNE IS PAVEd BY tHE NEWSPAPER SYNdiCATES

RECENTLY, I SHOWED MY COMIC STRIP to A MAJOR SYNdiCATION GUY IN NEW YORK

JUST A LittLE CRitiQUE, OKAY? NOtHiNG PERSONAL

FIRST, YOUR LEttERING IS tERRiBLE

I HATE LEttERING

SECOND, YOUR WRitiNG COULd USE ALOT OF HELP

I HATE WRitiNG

FURtHERMORE, YOUR LAYOUTS COULd BE ALOT MORE dYNAMiC

I HATE dYNAMiC

ANd tHE PREMiSE HAS **NO** MASS APPEAL

I HATE MASS APPEAL

WELL, EXCUSE ME, BUT iF YOU HATE dOiNG ALL OF tHiS, WHY did YOU EVEN **COME** HERE?

BECAUSE WHEN I GET HOME I'M GONNA HAVE FUN dRAWiNG YOU AS A BiG FAt UGLY dROOLiNG NAKEd MUSH-BRAINEd **GOON** ANd it'S GONNA BE iN WORCESTER MAGAZiNE!!

I HATE YOU

I LOVE tHAt

Len Peterson

TRIBUTE TO AMY

AMY →

We All Have A Friend Like My good friend AMY

She talks... **A lot**

Hi, AMY... How ARE You?

BLAH BLAH BLAH BLAH BLAH BLAH BLAH BLAH BLAH BLAH BLAH BLAH BLAH BLAH BLAH BLAH BLAH BLAH BLAH BLAH BLAH BLAH BLAH BLAH BLAH BLAH BLAH BLAH BLAH BLAH BLAH BLAH BLAH BLAH BLAH BLAH BLAH BLAH BLAH BLAH BLAH BLAH BLAH BLAH BLAH BLAH BLAH BLAH BLAH BLAH BLAH BLAH BLAH BLAH BLAH

I HAD A Meeting with one OF THE Hot shot NEWSPAPER Syndicate GUYS IN New York last week

MR. Peterson, I'M AFRAID WE'RE Not INTERESTED IN YOUR COMIC STRip... IN FACT, You should PROBABLY EVEN think ABOUT IF You could **HANDLE** A CAREER CREATING A COMIC STRip

Well, SIR... with people Like You IN MY Life, I'd **NEVER** RUN OUT OF MATERIAL

Thank You... that's VERY kind OF You to SAY...

HEY!!.. WAIT A MiNuTe!

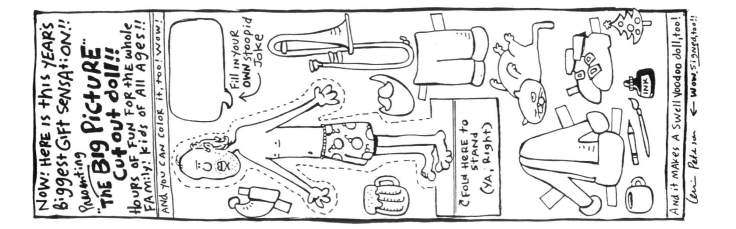

NOW! HERE IS THIS YEAR'S BIGGEST GIFT SENSATION!! Presenting "THE BIG PICTURE" Cut out doll!! Hours of fun FOR THE whole FAMILY! Kids of All AGES!! AND YOU CAN color it, too! WOW!

Fill IN YOUR OWN stoopid Joke

(Fold HERE to STAND (YA, Right)

And it makes A Swell Voodoo doll, too! ← WOW, Signed, too!!

It Ain't EASY Being A Future Big-TIME CARTOONIST

No matter what's going on in your Life you have to come up with something FUNNY EVERY day

Hmm... How 'Bout A Big Stoopid dog in UNFUNNY HUMAN situations Hmm

FOR INSTANCE, AS I WRITE this I've got the CHICKEN POX

Isn't this supposed to Be A Little kids illness as IN "CHICKEN POPS"?

I've Got PAINFUL, Stinging Red spots All over Me (AND I **do** MEAN **ALL** over)

ON MY BALD head — clothes hurt

ON MY hands (it hurts to draw!)

AND ON MY PRIVATE PARTS (hold newspaper at 90 degree Angle to see PRIVATE PARTS)

But I Always try to MAKE the BEST OF EVERYTHING

You've got Chicken POX

Cool...maybe I CAN get A CARTOON out OF it

Hi! I'M LENNIE PETERSON AND I'M HERE to tell YOU ABOUT the New CHICKEN POX FUN BOX BROUGHT to you by "the Big Picture"!

CONNECT the dots!

BOIL YOUR tea on the heat FROM YOUR OWN FEVER!

WHEEEEE!

CReate YOUR OWN LANGUAGE FROM the throBBing stabbing PAIN of the Pox wounds

YARGHEEE!!

THAT MEANS "SOMEBODY... PLEASE SHOOT ME"

THE Big PICTURE

by LENNIE "why don't you get A REAL JOB" PETERSON

Hi, kevin- it's Lennie

Hi, uncle Lennie- I **knew** it was you

that's so cool when that happens... do you think it's telepathy or the close family ties connecting our minds and spirits through generations of blood lines?

Caller I.d.

PRESENTING
the Big Picture

LENNIE MAKE OVER CONTEST

RECOVERED FROM THE CHICKEN POX, ITS TIME FOR A **NEW** LOOK!

1. USING the picture shown here, draw a new hair style on lennie's head!

2. NAME the new Look!

3. Send your entry to: The Big Picture c/o this NEWSPAPER

WINNERS will be published here, in your favorite newspaper! **WOW!** you'll be **FAMOUS!**

(DON'T FORGET to NAME it!)

OKAY, OKAY... I'll put this stoopid outfit on for you

COOL!

AND I'll EVEN let you chase me around the room and shoot me with your little bow and arrow

YESSS!

BUT I will **NOT** swing from that rope and sing "MY FUNNY VALENTINE"

DAMN

YOU'RE SO **UPTIGHT**

Response to this comic strip is best when the subject is either **COFFEE** or my 🐱 **CAT**

YUM!

Therefore, in the interest of my readers (and my interest in money) this strip will now be called "GINGER, the COFFEE CRAZED CAT." (formerly "the Big Picture")

GINGER WILL BE the STAR-

DECAF SUCKS!

She's no Heathcliff!

Now all I've gotta do is get her up to five cups a day

C'mon, little kitty... just a couple of bowls... we're gonna be rich and famous!

THEY'RE HERE! the WINNERS
OF the Big Picture LENNIE MAKE OVER CONTEST

thanks to all who entered...these are the best ones. The rest of 'em kinda stunk. But thanks anyway.

"THE EARWIG WIG"

Julie- Jefferson, MA.

"LAWNIE"

Simone- Seattle, WA.

"EAR WIG"

Misty- Apache Junction AZ.

"NANCY"

Robyn- Worcester, MA.

MORE WINNERS NEXT WEEK!! WHOA!! YIPPEE!!

Hey! ☆ MORE WINNERS!

(This is the LAST OF MY stoopid contest— I promise—what can I say? It did take up about 3 weeks worth of easy deadlines for me..)

L.P.

ROBYN Worcester. MA.

"PUNK-ADOUR"

DARLENE Worcester, MA.

THE ANT HILL (not the bee hive)
Cynthia WORCESTER, MA.

"MR. SOFTEE"

Mike Worcester. MA. (Worcester must be the place to be)

THANK YOU ALL FOR ENTERING! Please send more time consuming contest ideas!

The Big Picture

by Lennie "what?" Peterson

Hey, look! It's my ex-boyfriend, Robert!

OH YA

Hi, Beth!

OH BOY

Hi, Robert! You look GREAT! Jeez, have you been working out?

Little too much time on our hands there, BULK BOY?

I hear your retail outlets just went public and you also got appointed to the Board of Trustees at "The United Way"!

YA, but can he draw a decent looking CAT?

Are you still studying VAN GOGH?

C'mon...this guy's a friggin' "KEN" doll... Probably kisses like a two by four... That's why she dumped him probably... She needs someone SEXUAL like ME

ROBERT writes an advice column for "PLAYBOY"

So he's got everything but a sense of humor

I'm sorry... Where are my MANNERS? This is my boyfriend, Lennie

Hi! LOVE your comic strip, man... REALLY cool

Nice Guy!

The Big Picture

by Lennie "is this A CASH Gig?" Peterson

The Big Picture PRESENTS the WEDDING HALL OF FAME

HERE's A **TRUE** Fun Fact. As A Musician I've Played over ONE THOUSAND weddings! True!

CERTAIN Stoopid things happen at Most EVERY wedding:

AN idiot GROOM will Stuff CAKE in the BRiDE's FACE

SPLOTCH!

HA HA HA HA

AS A Joke, SOME CLOWN will dance with ANOTHER GUY... He thinks it's the FIRST TIME ANYONE HAS EVER thought OF this

HA HA HA HA HA HA HA HA*

*this ALWAYS Gets A Big LAUGH

there's ALWAYS A dRUNK, FAT "UNCLE SOMEBODY"

Meeshakoo?

Huh?

AND A MALL RAT COUSIN OF the GROOM

Hey... Like, dood... CAN't you PLAY some, Like, **GOOD** MUSIC?

And it's ALWAYS FUN to REMEMBER that FOR AN UGLY BRIDE And GROOM, it's the Best they'll EVER LOOK!

How'd you **do** it? How did you guys get in such great comic strips?

I'm constantly hustling **my** strip to all the newspaper syndicates, try to keep as "mainstream" as I can without selling out **and** I've written kiss-ass letters to all the right people in high places... How come I'm not rich and famous?

I THINK **I** KNOW WHAT'S WRONG

Really? What?

YOU'RE SUPPOSED TO BE **FUNNY**

DAMN

"dilbert" ©Scott Addams "CALVIN" © Bill Watterson "GRIMM" © Mike Peters

I RECENTLY HAD the PRIVILEGE OF WORKING WITH the GREAT **TONY BENNETT**

I played in the back-up band when he came through Boston

Cool

I'll NEVER FORGET HIS ADVICE to me

Hey, kid, move your TROMBONE CASE... I gotta get through there

ANOTHER honest to God true story FROM YOUR PALS AT "the Big Picture"

It happened IN the MEN'S ROOM AT A gig RECENTLY

HEY! AREN'T YOU the GUY IN that comic strip?!

He ACTUALLY WANTED to shake MY HAND right there AT the URINAL! **JEEZ!!**

UM...

WHAT comic strip?

ANOTHER
WORD-FOR-WORD
HONEST-to-PETE
TRUE STORY
FROM
YOUR PALS
AT
tHE
**Big
PicTuRE**

I took My dad out
to eat on FATHERS' day

Gee...this STEAK
IS **TOUGH**

EXCUSE ME...
This STEAK is **REALLY**
tough...I CAN BARELY
CuT through it

I'M SORRY

I'll GET YOU
A SHARPER KNIFE

It's SO CUTE how CATS
Like to STEAL PENS
AND PENCILS AND BAT
them All AROUND

it's ALSO CUTE how thEY
Like to Lie down on
PAPERS

ZZZ

it's ALMOST AS CUTE AS thE
MONEY I'M LOSING
BECAUSE OF it!!

**WHERE ARE
MY PENS??!**

HOSTAGES...EVERY
ONE OF 'EM

WOW...thESE HOROSCOPES
GET MORE AND MORE
ACCURATE

TAKE **YOURS**
FOR INSTANCE

Huh?

"IF YOU don't GET OFF YOUR
SORRY BUTT AND START PAYING
MORE AttENTion to thE GORGEOUS
BABE YOU'RE SITTING WITH,
SHE'S GOING TO LEAVE YOU FOR HER
BODY BUILDING-LIFEGUARD-
EX-BOYFRIEND BEFORE YOU CAN
SAY 'SCREW
WORKING ON thE
COMIC STRIP FOR
todAY, LET'S GO
OUT FOR dINNER'"

THE Big Picture

by Lennie "medium REGULAR ONE SUGAR" PETERSON

NOW!! SKIM PRECIOUS MOMENTS FROM YOUR VERY BUSY SCHEDULE EVERY DAY ON AMERICA'S SUPER HIGHWAYS!!

THE Big Picture PRESENTS the "DO·it·ALL·DASHBOARD" TIME SAVER Kit

dedicated to the Guy who SWERVED IN FRONT OF Me doing Eighty ON the MASS. Pike todAY while driving TALKING ON the PHONE And SHAVING All At ONCE! Such SkiLL! So BUSY! SO IMPORTANT!

I'M NOT GONNA READ this

C'MON, Beth.. It's IN the SCRipT FOR this week's Comic strip... People ARE READING this... Just SAY YOUR Line, OKAY?

ALRight, ALRight

"Lennie, YOU ARE SO SCARY-talented And SeXy I JUST WANT to Rip My Clothes OFF Right HERE AND NOW AND Let You HAVE YOUR WAY With ME"

I think I'm GONNA BARF

HEY! NO Ad LiB! That's Not IN My SCRipt!

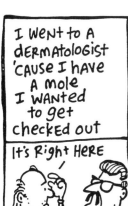

I WENT to a dermatologist 'CAUSE I have a mole I WANTED to get checked out

It's Right HERE

This doctor WAS ABOUT MY AGE (40ish) - He WORE A HORRIBLE Wig And his mustache WAS dyed Jet Black

That spot is HARMLESS... MANY people get those As they Get OLDER

CAN You Remove it FOR me?

I Could But...

He Actually SAid this-

Why don't You Just tRY to GROW old GRACEfully?

63

1st PLACE WINNER
the "SINGLE MOMS WHO NEED to GET OUT MORE" AWARD

JUST ONE MORE LOOK BEFORE WE GO...
I SWEAR to God Thumbelina's Voice is the SAME AS ARieL's FROM "the Little MERMAiD"... It's GOttA Be the SAME PERSON... I'm GONNA MAKE SOME CALLs TOMORROW AND check iNto it

YOU WANT SOME JUicy·Juice OR SomethiNg?

1st PLACE WINNER
CAtEGORY II "Single moms who Need to Get out more" AWARD

IF I ORDER the "HAPPY MEAL" CAN YOU BE SURE I get the Polly Pockets **HOUSE** AND NOt the Polly Pockets Ring? EVERY time My daughter AND I GO out **to EAt** WE ALWAYs Seem to end up with the Polly Pockets **Ring**

BACK WHEN I tAught At Berklee they used to send ME ON trips teaching AND PERFORMiNg... I went to JAPAN, ITALY, SPAIN, ARGENTiNA AND All OVER the StAtes

COFFEE, PLEASE
AND BEER too

I LEARNED A VALUABLE LESSON IN All those trAVELs - that PEOPLE, FOR BEtter OR WORSE, ARE BASICALLY the SAme ANYWHERE YOU GO...

CAts too

I LIKE YOUR CAt!

SHE NO CARE

THE BIG PICTURE
THE BIG PICTURE
THE BIG PICTURE
THE BIG PICTURE
THE BIG PICTURE
THE BIG PICTURE

by Lennie

"Oh, YA? I bet I could kick YOUR Butt iN 'Pictionary'..."

Peterson

I'M sick OF HEARiNG All that Cliché "GUY" stuff that's FoRCed DoWN OUR throats

FIRST OF All, I KNOW PLENTY OF GUYS, INCLUDING me, that HAVE **NO** PROBLEM ASKING FOR DIRECTIONS

TRUE

Second, I AM COMPLETELY CONSIDERATE AS FAR AS PUTTING the toilet SEAT BACK doWN

That's true...I APPRECIATE that

And third, I do **NoT** think ONLY OF SPORTS, sex ANd BEER

And third, I do **NoT** think ONLY OF SPORTS

today sucks

Response to Last week's Comic Strip has been INTERESTING

SOME people thought it was too "LOCAL" in REFERENCE—UM, FOLKS...the strip is About my Life And I Live NEAR PARK Ave. IN WORCESTER... OKAY?

The MOST INTERESTING was the difference IN OPINION BeTween MEN AND WOMEN Although I hAD NO INTENTION FOR it to CONTRIBUTE to the BATTLE of the SEXES— I REALLY don't think that WAY At All

Most men loved it. Most women HAted it

it WAS SO INSULTING... It BRINGS Attention to you MEN'S LACK OF SENSITIVITY AND INABILITY FOR INTIMACY

REALLY, I WAS Just hoping to BRING Attention to the PAIN- IN-THE-ASS pot- holes on PARK AVE. IN WORCESTER

You're All the SAME

Hey, LENNIE! GREAT STRIP LASt week!

Hints that the HONEYMOON is over
HINT #63

I keep hAving this Nightmare where SKINNY, BALD-headed SPACE ALIENS CAPTURE ME AND BRING ME BACK to THEIR PLANET. They hold ME CAPTIVE AND WORK NON-STOP, COMPLETELY IGNORING ME. And THEY BRAIN-WASH ME telling ME that Someday I'll Be the QUEEN of THEIR WORLD IF I JUST Agree to STAY. The Aliens keep PROMISING ME the LIVING conditions will improve But they NEVER do. Finally, A hANDSOME EARTHLING PRINCE COMES Along, dePROGRAMS ME AND whisks ME AWAY BACK down to EARTh to Live hAPPily EVER After

Hmm... what do you suppose that means?

THE BIG PICTURE

by Lennie "white out" Peterson

It's that **WORD** everybody's using... anywhere, anytime for **anything!**

My theory is that it all started with **CATS** - they've known "THE WORD" for **CENTURIES**

I love you, kitty... you're my best friend in the whole world!

whatever

It's the new **Etiquette**

Thank you very much - have a great day!

Whatever

Unfortunately, it can even come up in your **LOVE LIFE** *

Was it good for **YOU?**

Whatever

*OKAY... MY LOVE LIFE

One more week * of that **MAGIC WORD** - use it anywhere, anytime!! it's so **EASY!**

*SEE LAST WEEK - OR WHATEVER

In the halls of **Justice** -

How do you plead? Guilty or not Guilty?

WHATEVER

In the Halls of **medicine** -

Give it to me straight, Doc... how bad is it?

WHATEVER

In my hall - just last night, in fact -

WHAT?! You've been cheating on me and now you're leaving me for him? but I can't live without you!!

whatever

WHAT?! You're actually dumping me for **Him?** But he's an **idiot**, Beth!

I can't **believe** this! What about our history? Our passion? Our **fire?** What about our connection to each other? Our plans? My relationship with your daughter? What does **HE** have that **I** don't **have??**

A real **JOB?**

Bingo

this week's comic strip
has been cancelled.
Nothing's Funny
Right Now.

Hey. It happens.

Hey. Everybody!
It's
Contest
TiME!!

DRAW **YOUR**
VERSION
OF the Big Dopey
Macho Dork
with the REAL JOB
that my
GIRLFRieND
Left me FOR!!
(WINNERS WiLL BE
Published heRE!!)

YOU CAN
NAME
him too!!
WOW!

ACCESSORIES INCLUDE:

Corvette

PERFECT
HAIR

Big house

Big dopey
+ruck

Big muscles-he wants
to BEAT me up!

Send Entries to "the Big Picture Contest" CARE OF this Noosepaper...WINNERS WiLL RECEiVE
A "Big Picture" original FROM YouR FAVORite Bitter, Jealous, psycho CARTOONist/musiciAN!!

this
Episode
we
Jump
Ahead
to +he
Year
1998!

☆ **STARRING**:☆
my ex-girlfriend
And the Big dopey
Macho dork with
the REAL JOB
that my Ex-girl-
FRieND Left
me FOR

Hi, Honey,
How WAS
YOUR dAY?

Hmmph

PSSSt

Honey...
do you
Love ME?

Hmmph

Honey?

Why didn't
I stAy with
LENNiE
PETERSON?

Hmmph

PSSSSt

NEXT EPISODE: 1999!

THE BIG PICTURE

by Lennie "this sure beats working for a living" Peterson

NOW! BY POPULAR DEMAND!*
introducing this cartoonist's
CREATIVE PROCESS

(*Actually, nobody "demanded" at all. Nobody even asked... But, it DOES take care of my cartoon for this week)

STEP #1 — the HARVESTING of CREATIVE thought

STEP #2 — The ORGANIZATION AND VISUALIZATION OF CONCEPT AND ARTISTIC FORMAT

STEP #3 — INSPIRATION STRIKES FROM DEEP WITHIN THE HEART AND SOUL OF THE COSMIC GRID

Riiiiiing

LENNIE, its Allen FROM the "HOMESTEADER" MAGAZINE...IF YOU don't MAKE YOUR DEADLINE THIS MONTH WE'RE dropping YOUR stoopid CARTOON FOR GOOD...I don't CARE WHO you ARE!!

STEP #4 — RENDERING BEGINS, RESULTING IN BRILLIANT ACHIEVEMENT OF ARTISTIC INTEGRITY

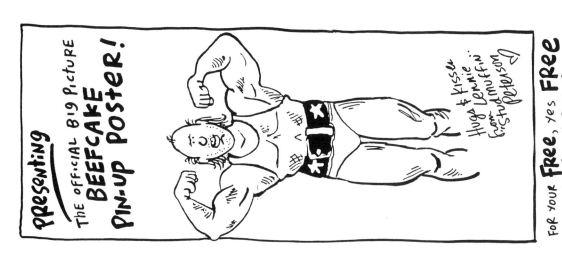

Please note:
1. Last month's contest has been cancelled
2. The brilliant and funny 10 week series, "Lennie gets dumped," has been officially discontinued
3. I'm a sorry-assed wimp
4. It's just a comic strip
5. I give up. Thank you

But it was FUNNY

Uh oh... Lennie's defending yet another comic strip to yet another editor

He should just give them my special evil voodoo curse from Hell

May you return in your next life as a skinny bald middle aged cartoonist/trombonist

That's it... I'm SICK of the lawsuit threats... what a bunch of CRAP

Maybe I won't include any real people in my comic strip anymore... apparently NO one has a sense of HUMOR around here

From now on maybe it's just my cat and ME

Actually, I'M holding out 'till Cartoon Boy gets syndicated... Then I'll sue for a lifetime supply of Fancy Feast and a place of my own

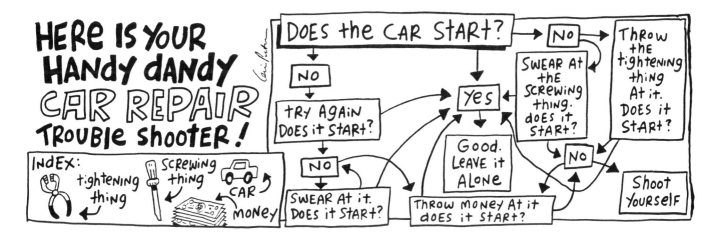

HERE IS YOUR HANDY DANDY CAR REPAIR TROUBLE SHOOTER!

INDEX:
tightening thing
screwing thing
car
money

DOES the CAR START?

NO → SWEAR at the SCREWING thing. does it START? → NO → Throw the tightening thing at it. DOES it START?

NO
TRY AGAIN DOES it START?
NO
SWEAR at it. DOES it START?

YES

Good. LEAVE it ALONE

THROW MONEY at it does it START?

NO

Shoot yourself

73

the big picture

by LENNIE "but what's your REAL JOB?" PETERSON

The other day I was sitting in front of GIANT OFFICE BUILDINGS filled with GUYS IN SUITS walking in and out all AFTERNOON

EVERYBODY LOOKED **REALLY** BUSY

And they **All** looked like they'd rather be doing something else

I STARTED WONDERING IF something FUNNY HAPPENS to **EVERY**body everyday like it does to ME But they just don't have a comic strip to express it in like **I** do

THEN I STARTED WONDERING IF MAYbe I HAVE too much time on my hands

74

She was perfect for me in every way

There will never be another like her

Sure, she had some problems... but I always loved her uncondit·onally

Painful as it is, we all must learn to let go

Rest in Peace, My Nissan Pulsar
1987-96

I'm sorry, Mr. Peterson- we can't give you a car loan

Huh? Why not?

Truthfully, Mr. Peterson, your credit .....sucks

WHAT?

My **CREDIT?!** Listen, pal! Perhaps you don't know who you're talkin' to! I'm gonna be a big time cartoonist someday so don't you worry one **bit** about my **CREDIT!** now give me that **LOAN!**

There's no built-in coffee cup holder for my coffees to go

Oh, no

SALE

Lennie...You've been car shopping for three weeks now.. This car is perfect- It's fully loaded at a **GREAT** price

With no built-in coffee cup holder for his coffee to go

P.S. GOT ONE

LENNIE, SOMEONE OUT THERE WANTS TO MEET YOU

DRESSING ROOM

IS IT A TATTOOED BIKER CHICK WITH A PIERCED TONGUE WEARING A LEATHER MINISKIRT AND FISH-NET STOCKINGS?

UM... NO

I'M NOT HERE

Good NEWS EVERYBODY!

THIS VERY COMIC STRIP "THE BiG PICTURE" JUST WON **FiRST PLACE** IN "EdiToriAL HUMOR" MAGAZiNE'S NATionwidE CONTEST FOR Best Comic Strip!!

IT WAS JUDGED BY A PANEL OF BiG TiME SYNDICATED CARTOONISTS INCLUDING ONE OF MY TWO FAVORiTE CARTOONISTS OF ALL TiME, **TOM TOLES!***

* WHOA!

AND THERE'S ABSOLUTELY **NO** NEED TO WORRY

DAD?...

I WON'T FORGET **ANYONE**

...TAKE A LEFT ON SUNSET

SOMETIMES THE THINGS I DRAW IN THiS COMIC STRIP ACTUALLY COME TRUE IN REAL LiFE AFTER THEY'RE PUBLISHED!

FOR INSTANCE, **this** ACTUALLY HAPPENED ONE WEEK AFTER iT APPEARED HERE

WHAT-EVER

THiS CAME TRUE JUST **two dAys** AFTER iT WAS PUBLISHED

THERE'S ONLY ONE THiNG LEFT TO DO

The Big Picture

by Lennie "Whaddaya, Live in a Barn?" Peterson

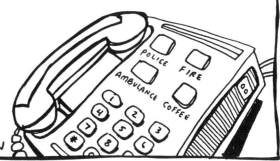

When I was a kid, my mother and father used to have this thing about keeping the refrigerator door open for more than about twenty seconds

Shut that door!!

Maybe it was a thing left over from the depression??

Or maybe their parents had ice boxes or something and the ice would melt if you kept the door open too long and yelling to shut the door just became habit

Shut that door!

But the way I figure it, even if you keep a refrigerator door open twenty **minutes**, I don't think the food will spoil

I never asked my father about this 'cause I think he'd be offended

Are you saying we didn't do a good job raising you or what?

Now that I'm an adult, when I really want to live on the edge I keep the refrigerator door open a full **minute**

HA!

77

Row 1:

File UNDER "I" FOR "I couldn't Make this stuff up IF I tried"

I went to my sister's house this morning

My sister (one of 'em..)

I opened the refrigerator to see if she had any cream

Shut that door!!

Row 2:

Jeez, Lennie... you've gotta try to move on now

Life is short, man... try to forgive and forget

Besides.. time heals ALL wounds

Ya... I know all that... It's just rough, okay?

He still misses "Calvin and Hobbes"

Row 3:

I think I'd like to be in a relationship again

So I took out a personal ad

SEEKING SINGLE WHITE FEMALE SOULMATE WITH CHARACTER · WILLING TO COMMIT TO GOOD TIMES & BAD INCLUDING MUSICIAN/ ARTIST LIFESTYLE. MUST BE INTELLIGENT, LOVING, TRUSTWORTHY, SENSITIVE, FUNNY, LAID-BACK & ABLE TO GIVE & TAKE UNCONDITIONALLY. ANIMAL INSTINCTS, LOVE OF KIDS, PETS, FINE FOODS, A STRONG SEX DRIVE, SLEEPING IN, AND HANGING OUT TOGETHER AT HOME A BIG PLUS.

then I realized my prayers for that ad were answered LONG ago

It's just not EXActly what I had in mind

Panel 1: MY NEPHEW TODD IS FIGHTING LEUKEMIA* YET HE EATS LIKE HORSE... HE STAYED OVERNIGHT LAST NIGHT

* HE'S DOIN' REAL GOOD...

Todd

Panel 2: I OFFERED HIM A NUTTY BUDDY ICE CREAM CONE*

Nutty Buddy

* I LOVE NUTTY BUDDIES

Panel 3: HE SAID HE DOESN'T LIKE NUTTY BUDDIES

I DON'T LIKE NUTTY BUDDIES

Panel 4: I LOOKED IN MY FREEZER THIS MORNING. ALL THE NUTTY BUDDIES WERE GONE

Panel 5: THIS IS A TRUE STORY WORD FOR WORD

I WAS TELLING MY FRIENDS THAT I MET YOU

REALLY?

Panel 6: I WAS TELLING THEM HOW YOU REMIND ME OF THAT ARTIST

WHO?... PICASSO? WHO?

Panel 7: NO, NOT PICASSO... YOU KNOW... UM

WHO? ESCHER? DALI? WHO?

Panel 8: CAROLINE IN THE CITY!!

Panel 9: YOU THINK TWO CAREERS ARE TOUGH TO MANAGE? I HAD AT LEAST TWENTY-ONE!

Panel 10: TEACHER, MAID, CHEF, DOCTOR, HOUSEKEEPER, FUND-RAISER, BUTLER, FASHION DESIGNER, CHAUFFER, ACCOUNTANT, NUTRITIONIST, DIPLOMAT, CAREER COUNCILOR, NURSE, BANKER, NANNIE, PLUMBER, CARPENTER, ACTIVITIES DIRECTOR AND THERAPIST!

Panel 11: WHAT ARE YOU TALKING ABOUT? YOU WERE OUR MOM

Panel 12: HAPPY MOTHERS' DAY, EVERYBODY

OH

APPRECIATE YOURS!

the BiG PiCture

BY LENNIE "I FORGOT MY WALLET" PETERSON

I'M DRAWING THIS FROM A PLANE...
I'M BEING FLOWN TO KANSAS CITY
FOR A MEETING THAT COULD
MEAN
Big STUFF
FOR THIS COMIC STRIP!*

*YEEHA! I GOT NOTICED BY UNIVERSAL PRESS SYNDICATE!!!

BUT RIGHT NOW IT'S 6:30 A.M.
AND ALL I CAN THINK
ABOUT IS HOW TO GET
A
Stoopid
CUP OF COFFEE

AND IF THE STOOPID FLIGHT
ATTENDANT DOESN'T GET OFF
HER STOOPID SORRY ASS
PRETTY SOON THERE'S GONNA
BE A
Hi-JACKING!

KANSAS City. DAY ONE

FROM START TO FINISH, "UNIVERSAL PRESS SYNDICATE" TREATED ME LIKE ROYALTY

WOW! A WINDOW SEAT?

I'M NOT ACCUSTOMED TO THAT KIND OF THING

COOL! A LIMO! CAN I SIT UP FRONT WITH YOU?

BUT I FINALLY ADJUSTED —

ALSO, IF YOU DON'T DELIVER THOSE BLACK OLIVES UP HERE **PRONTO** HEADS WILL ROLL, HEAR ME ??!! AND NO **PITS** THIS TIME !!

to BE CONTINUED —

KANSAS City DAY two (with the V.P.)

JEEZ, HE'S BEING **REALLY** NICE TO ME BUT, STILL, I'M SO NERVOUS I COULD THROW UP

UNIVERSAL PRESS SYNDICATE
LEE SALEM V.P.

IF I DRAW HIM NAKED WITH A BIG GOOFY NOSE AND A FUNNY HAT IT MIGHT MAKE ME FEEL BETTER

BUT, THEN AGAIN, IF HE SEES HIM- SELF LIKE THAT IN MY COMIC STRIP HE'LL **NEVER** OFFER ME A CONTRACT

I'd BETTER NOT

LEE SALEM V.P.

KANSAS City DAY 3

discussions with UNIVERSAL PRESS SYNDICATE seem to be going well

DO YOU HAVE AN AGENT?

A LAWYER?

NO

NO

ANY REPRESENTATION WHATSOEVER?

NO

ANY CLUE HOW TO EVEN READ A CONTRACT?

NO

YOU'RE DESPERATE, AREN'T YOU?

WANNA BUY MY WATCH?

KANSAS CiTY DAY 4

PEOPLE OUT HERE think I TALK FUNNY SO I'm HiRiNG AN iNTERPRETER to TRANSLATE MY NEW ENGLAND ACCENT

Jeet yet?

Huh?

He SAiD "Did you eAT yET?"

Oh!... No... did you?

Notchyet! Squeet!

Huh?

I CAN'T WAiT to get HOME to MY CAT... SHE MUST MiSS ME SOMETHiNG TERRiBLE

BEAUTiFUL iTALiAN WiFE OF FAT SLOBBY RiCH GUY

IF CARTOON BOY LEAVES ME WiTH tHiS CRAPPY **DRY** FOOD FOR THREE DAYS EVER AGAiN, HiS NEW SOFA BECOMES MY OWN PERSONAL "HAiRBALL HABiTAT"

THREE REASONS I LOVE MY CAT (MAYBE MORE THAN ANYThiNG ELSE)

1 SHE **MEDITATES** BETTER THAN I DO

2 SHE **SHEDS** AS MUCH AS I DO

Jeesh

Jeesh

3 SHE'S THE RECLUSE I'VE ALWAYS WANTED TO BE

I'M GOiN' OUT

THAT'S **STOOPID**

THE BIG PICTURE

BY LENNIE (LATE CHARGE) PETERSON

FUZZ BUCKET

CARTOON BOY

Now that I'm thinking about it, maybe my meeting with the syndicate didn't go so well after all*

Hi!

UPS

V.P.

*they haven't called back

OKAY, so y'see, MY comic strip is all about **ME** and MY life and, y'know, being an artist and musician and stuff and coffee and stuff

And there's my cat, Ginger!

ZZZ

And it's, y'know, um...

Stuff that happens

to me

And stuff

Would it help my chances if I change Ginger's name to "Catbert"?

[4] SHE'S A GREAT JUDGE OF CHARACTER

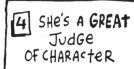

I'M SORRY... YOU HAVE to LEAVE... GINGER DOESN'T LIKE YOU

[5] SHE NEVER ARGUES MY LiFE'S PHILOSOPHIES

AND SO, Y'SEE? EVERYTHING IS NORMALLY A COINCIDENCE!

[6] I ASPIRE to HER LiFESTYLE OF EATING, SLEEPING AND KEEPING STRANGE HOURS

WAKE UP, CARTOON BOY... TIME to SCRATCH MY BELLY

LET ME GET THIS STRAIGHT, EINSTEIN

YOU HAD A MEETING WITH ONE OF THE LARGEST SYNDICATES IN THE WORLD AND YOU'RE NOT HOUNDING THEM FOR A RESPONSE!? YOU ARE CRAZY!

HEY! I'M AN ARTIST, TEESHA... NOT EVERY-THING IS ABOUT MONEY Y'KNOW

NOW LET'S JUST ENJOY OUR MACARONI AND KETCHUP, SHALL WE?

ARE YOU TEESHA?

PROBABLY

I THOUGHT YOU SHOULD KNOW YOUR BOYFRIEND HERE MADE A PASS AT ME LAST NIGHT... HE ACTUALLY ASKED ME to HAVE SEX WITH HIM

YOU SHOULD GO FOR IT

IT'LL BE THE BEST THIRTY SECONDS OF YOUR LIFE

I'm working really hard on my spiritual growth

Reading, thinking, meditating, soul-searching and seeking happiness from the inside-out

Today, it dawned on me that all along **she** has been trying to teach me the simple answer to the problems and confusion we encounter in this life and the path to complete, inner peace

Took you long enough

NAPS

And plenty of 'em

There is still no conclusion to my syndication saga

$

But my girlfriend said (and this is an exact quote):

I'm probably gonna dump you if you don't get syndicated

I laughed and said:

No, really...

She said:

No, really- I'm probably gonna dump you if you don't get syndicated

She also told me if I ever put her in this comic strip again, she wouldn't speak to me

Fortunately for me, she's always kept her word

BAD NEWS, EVERYBODY.. UNIVERSAL PRESS SYNDICATE HAS TURNED DOWN MY COMIC STRIP FOR SYNDICATION...

THEY SAID THEY REALLY **LIKE** MY STRIP BUT CAN'T QUITE FIND A MARKET FOR IT

I'M SO BUMMED OUT... MY RENT IS LATE AGAIN, MY GIRLFRIEND'S MAD AT ME AND MY COMIC STRIP HAS BEEN REJECTED BY UNIVERSAL PRESS

I KNOW WHAT YOU MEAN... I'VE BEEN KIND OF BUMMED OUT MY**SELF** LATELY

BIG DEAL... ALL YOU HAVE IS **LEUKEMIA**

LIFE GOES ON...

SORT OF

SO WHAT? YOU DIDN'T GET SYNDICATED... THERE'S OTHER STUFF YOU CAN DO INSTEAD

YA... LIKE LAY HERE DEPRESSED TILL I **DIE**

CAN I HAVE YOUR CAT?

I WONDER HOW LENNIE'S HANDLING BEING REJECTED BY THE SYNDICATE

HMM... I DUNNO. I HAVEN'T HEARD FROM HIM

OH, WELL.. HE'S BEEN IN MUSIC AND ART LONG ENOUGH TO KNOW HOW TO DEAL WITH REJECTION.. I'M SURE HE'S BOUNCED RIGHT BACK BY NOW

AND THEN, BROTHER LEONARD, AFTER OUR DAILY FIVE HOUR MEDITATION, WE HAVE OUR BREAKFAST OF TOFU CAKES AND WATER

Substitute teaching...

AGAIN

So, if a B-flat major triad is constructed with a **MAJOR** third on the bottom, it stands to reason that a B-flat **MINOR** triad would be constructed with a minor third on the bottom

Any questions? Yes?

do you think Scott Weiland will ever get back together with "Stone Temple Pilots"?

THEY'RE AWESOME

YOU'RE INCREDIBLE!

SO HANDSOME... SO CREATIVE...AND SO VERY **SEXY** AND BEST OF ALL, YOU'RE A **CARTOONIST!** OOOH!...

HEY!... DO WE HAVE ANY "FRISKY KITTY TREATS" LEFT?

Huh?

P O O F

DING DONG

TRICK OR TREAT

TRICK OR TREAT

THE BIG PICTURE

by Lennie "Sumner" Peterson

there's another syndicate that's really interested in me but I don't think I'm interested in them... they're starting to say really **Stoopid** stuff

Do you plan on introducing more characters?*

CHARACTERS?

*Like I have a plan for **ANY**thing

OR:

We enjoy your self-deprecating approach but we think the "musician" angle without the self reference yet keeping the autobiographical twist along with the changes we discussed earlier would be much more appropriate for our demographic base

Huh?

OR:

Some of your writing is too risqué.. you have to use "heck" for the word "hell"

But it's about **real life**... who the hell talks like that, Little Billy from "the family circus"?

Then **I** say stoopid stuff

This one about your car is really funny

That one's not funny at all

LOUISE'S MOM, YOLANDE, PASSED AWAY YESTERDAY. SHE HAD CANCER

LOUISE IS MY EX-WIFE →

SHE WAS ONE OF THE KINDEST, MOST LOVING AND SELFLESS PEOPLE YOU COULD MEET. THE KIND OF PERSON YOU'D NEVER WANT TO DISAPPOINT.

BEFORE SHE DIED, YOLANDE TOLD LOUISE SHE'D BE WATCHING US ALL FROM BEHIND THE MOON

FOR THE REST OF MY LIFE I'LL NEVER LOOK AT THE MOON IN THE SAME WAY. MAYBE YOU WON'T EITHER

BE NICE TO EACH OTHER. YOLANDE IS WATCHING.

REST IN PEACE, YOLANDE LAFONTAINE (1925-1997) YOUR LOVE WAS UNCONDITIONAL

WOW... THAT'S REALLY GOOD!

That's GOOD?!

ONE OF MY FINE ART DRAWINGS JUST GOT ACCEPTED INTO A MUSEUM IN CALIFORNIA AND ALL **YOU** HAVE TO SAY IS "that's **GOOD**"?!

HOW MANY OF YOUR DOPEY LITTLE ARTSY FRIENDS CAN YOU SAY HAVE THEIR WORKS IN A **MUSEUM**, huh??

JEEZ...that's "GOOD"

IF ONLY MY DOPEY LITTLE ARTSY FRIENDS COULD BE AS **HUMBLE** AS YOU

WHAT?!

Nothing

MY COMIC STRIP WAS REJECTED BY UNIVERSAL PRESS BUT I THINK THAT **OTHER** SYNDICATE IS STILL INTERESTED

THE VICE PRESIDENT WANTS ME TO MAKE A LOT OF CHANGES IN THE STRIP THOUGH

YOUR CAT SHOULD BE A **DOG**

huh?

HE SAID HE **LIKES** THE STRIP BUT IT MIGHT NOT BE "MAINSTREAM" ENOUGH *

***WHATEVER THAT MEANS**

I'M TRYING TO PLAY IT COOL, SO I'M NOT CALLING HIM UNTIL HE CALLS ME...Y'KNOW, PLAY "HARD TO GET"- MAKE **HIM** SWEAT

GEE, IT'S **HOT**... HONEY, CAN YOU GRAB ME ANOTHER COLD ONE? I'M **SWEATING!**

THE Big PiCture

by LENNIE
"I STARTED
LOSING it the
day I MET
you"
- PETERSON

THE BiG PiCTURE - OVER 7 SOLD!!

DRIVE THRU

PRESENTING
the **SAGA**
OF MY **HAiR**
PAST PRESENT + FUTURE
(with Apologies to Howard Stern)

1957

1967

1977

1987

1997

2007

2017

2027

(SEE 1957)

WISHING YOU A BIG TIME HOLIDAY FROM ALL OF US AT "THE BIG PICTURE"! AND THANKS

HEY! REMEMBER LAST YEARS AWESOME BEEFCAKE PIN-UP POSTER? THIS YEAR WE PRESENT THE Big Picture SWIM SUIT PIN-UP POSTER!!

Jeesh...the things I've gotta do just so cartoon boy can make his Rent

THE BIG PICTURE

HAVE A GREAT YEAR!... AND THANKS FOR READING MY STOOPID COMIC STRIP

MY NEW YEAR'S RESOLUTION IS TO FINALLY GET A HAIR TRANSPLANT

① Chicks will dig it

Ooh, Lennie... Let us run our fingers through your plugs!

② I can stop seeing my therapist

...And the only reason you're attracted to tattooed biker chicks with pierced tongues wearing leather miniskirts and fishnet stockings is because you think your family hates you 'cause you're bald

Really?

③ People will finally stop referring to me as "The Bald Guy in the Band"

He's the guy in the band with the silly looking hair transplant

Oh, him

CARLA - ARE YOU AWAKE?

AM NOW

I had this really great dream... I had a full head of beautiful white hair!!

CLICK

GO BACK TO SLEEP

(THANKS, MONICA)

IT WAS JUST A DREAM

Z

EVENTUALLY, THE ANCIENT EGYPTIANS TURNED THE FELINE INTO SYMBOLS OF DEITIES

THE CAT BECAME REVERED AND WORSHIPPED AS A SACRED SYMBOL OF RELIGION

ENJOYING THE SPOILS AND RICHES OF ROYALTY, THE CAT WAS RE- GARDED AS "THE PERFECT GOD"

LET ME GUESS... YOU'VE BEEN WATCHING THE HISTORY CHANNEL AGAIN?

FOR THOSE OF YOU JUST JOINING US I'D LIKE TO TELL YOU A LITTLE ABOUT MY COMIC STRIP

ZZZ

THIS IS ME, AND THIS IS MY CAT GINGER AND IT'S ALL TRUE STUFF ABOUT US!

YOU WERE EXPECTING MAYBE BARFY AND DOLLY ROMPING THROUGH THE NEIGHBORHOOD WITH LITTLE BILLY?

 **THE BIG PICTURE** by LENNIE "RAMA" PETERSON

I like **this** comic strip

≡AACK≡

WHAT?! that comic strip is so predictable and **SAFE**... so **BLAND**...it's total NO-RISK, COOKIE CUTTER PRE-FAB MAIN STREAM **CRAP!**

It's just another stoopid strip drawn by the stoopid son or assistant of a stoopid dead cartoonist

Now, take **MY** comic strip for instance... **MY** comic strip is **REAL** and **INNOVATIVE** and from the **HEART**

I like **this** comic strip

CARLA...I'M SORRY, OUR RELATIONSHIP ISN'T WORKING... I STILL HAVEN'T RECOVERED FROM MY LAST ONE

Jeez... Get OVER it

I think it's a good idea if I don't see you anymore

YOU'RE BREAKING UP WITH ME?!

Better than that- I'm whiting you out!

dAMN...

Love SUCKS

Jeez...get OVER it

SOMETIMES, LIKE IN SEATTLE FOR WHATEVER REASON, IT GETS TO BE A FULL EIGHT INCHES LONG! VERY EXCITING!

Yet, IN SOME PLACES, LIKE WORCESTER, MA. AND APACHE JUNCTION, ARIZONA, I SHRINK DOWN TO AS LITTLE AS FOUR INCHES!! VERY HUMILIATING

Hey...

I WAS TALKING ABOUT THE SIZE MY COMIC STRIP IS PRINTED

Jeesh... YOUR MIND IS IN THE GUTTER

EVERY MUSICIAN HAS A LATE NIGHT DRUNK DRIVING STORY FROM THE OLD DAYS... MY FRIEND LARRY HAS A FRIEND WHO WAS CLOCKED IN THE LEFT HAND PASSING LANE OF THE MASS. PIKE

THE COP PULLED HIM OVER AND SAID:

DO YOU KNOW HOW FAST YOU WERE GOING?

LARRY'S FRIEND SAID:

UM... I dUNNO.. Eighty Five? Ninety?

the cop SAid:

Nope...

Fourteen

96

Row 1:

MY FRIEND MONICA'S SON SAW MY NEPHEW AND ME ON T.V. LAST WEEK

WHO'S THAT GUY WITH LENNIE?

THAT'S HIS NEPHEW TODD

HOW COME TODD'S GOT NO HAIR?

BECAUSE HE WAS VERY SICK WITH LEUKEMIA AND THE MEDICINE MADE HIS HAIR FALL OUT

WHAT MEDICINE DOES LENNIE TAKE?

Row 2:

I KEEP HEARING RUMORS* THAT I'M SUPPOSEDLY GETTING MARRIED!!

I DON'T EVEN HAVE A GIRLFRIEND**

* TRUE
** TRUE AGAIN

I'D LIKE TO MARRY MYSELF BUT I DON'T KNOW IF THAT'S LEGAL IN MASSACHUSETTS

DO YOU TAKE YOURSELF TO BE YOUR LAWFULLY WEDDED SELF?

I DO

OR MAYBE I SHOULD MARRY MY CAT GINGER

NOT WITHOUT A PRE-NUP, CARTOON BOY

COME TO THINK OF IT, MY BIOLOGICAL CLOCK IS TICKING... DO YOU THINK WOMEN WOULD BE OFFENDED IF I JUST CUT TO THE CHASE?

HEY! YOU'RE KINDA CUTE... WANNA HAVE MY BABIES?

TOLL BOOTH

Row 3:

SO, TRACY, WANNA COME UP FOR A DRINK?

SURE

HERE YOU GO

THANKS!

SLAM

THE BIG PICTURE

by Lennie "who are you?" Peterson

MY FATHER CONDUCTS THE ALETHIA GROTTO BAND HERE IN CENTRAL MASSACHUSETTS

NOW AND THEN HE ASKS ME IF I CAN SUBSTITUTE FOR HIS REGULAR TROMBONE PLAYER... SOMETIMES I CAN.

UM...OKAY

HE GIVES ME THE TIME AND DATE BUT THEN HE ALWAYS THINKS HE HAS TO CALL TO REMIND ME—

WHEN DO YOU WANT ME TO CALL AND REMIND YOU?

DAD—I'M FORTY YEARS OLD— I'VE BEEN PLAYING PROFESSIONALLY FOR TWENTY FIVE YEARS, HELPED TO RAISE A FAMILY, TAUGHT COLLEGE, I'VE RECORDED AND PERFORMED AROUND THE WORLD AND MY ARTWORK IS **EVERYWHERE**... DO YOU REALLY THINK YOU NEED TO CALL AND REMIND ME ABOUT YOUR **CONCERT**?

WHEN DO YOU WANT ME TO CALL AND REMIND YOU?

I'm LEAVING FOR HAWAii NEXT WEEK. I HAVE A gig THERE. It'll BE **GREAT**

WHAT A **DORK**

I'm going with A BAND FROM MINNEAPOLIS— the money's pretty good, too...

GREAT... IN THE MEANTIME, I'M STUCK HERE in WORCESTER with FOUR BOWLS OF DRY FOOD AND THE two MENTAL PATIENTS * IN THE APARTMENT DOWNSTAIRS CHECKING IN ON ME EVERY THREE DAYS

* THANKS JENN + ANNIE

...ENOUGH FOR A FOUR MONTH SUPPLY OF "FANCY FEAST"!

TEN POINTS FOR THE DORK

IN THE TRADITION OF "LITTLE BILLY" FROM THAT DOPEY COMIC STRIP "THE FAMILY CIRCUS," MY CAT GINGER WILL TAKE OVER THIS WEEK'S DUTIES OF CREATING <u>MY</u> COMIC STRIP WHILE I'M IN HAWAII

I AiN't DOiN' <u>SQUAT</u>...

Little Billy © B:I KEANE

HAWAII WAS GREAT. NOW I'M IN CHICAGO

Hi! WISH YOU WERE HERE!...

SOME OF YOU

I met this GUY, AL, AND HIS WiFE, JEAN. They READ this COMIC STRIP IN ONE OF THE ALTERNATIVE PAPERS OUT HERE—

That's SO COOL that you get MY COMIC STRIP OUT HERE!

LENNIE... WE **READ** YOUR COMIC STRIP...

NOBODY **"GETS"** YOUR COMIC STRIP

LAST WEEK WAS A WEEK OF NON-STOP TRAVELING, EXHAUSTION AND JET LAG.

LET'S MEET HERE AT FIVE.

UM... WHAT YEAR IS THIS?

AND BAD AIRPLANE FOOD—

I SWEAR TO GOD IT MOVED!

PERFORMING WITH WHINING, SELF-ABSORBED PRIMA DONNA LEAD SINGERS

THE LIMO WAS FIVE MINUTES LATE AND NOW I'M TOO UPSET TO SING!

Jeeziz

I SHOULDA BEEN A CAT

POSITION'S FILLED, CARTOON BOY... GET YOUR OWN LIFE

I MET A LADY ON THE STREET WHO KNEW MY MOM BEFORE SHE DIED

SHE SAID I'VE GOT MY MOTHER'S SMILE

THANKS

LITTLE DOES SHE KNOW THAT I'VE GOT MUCH MUCH MORE

BYE

I'VE GOT MY **MOM**

HAPPY MOTHERS' DAY EVERYONE

MAY YOU ALWAYS HAVE YOURS

THREE WAYS I'LL BE COMMEMORATING MY BIG BIRTHDAY THIS WEEK

① I'M ADDING A LINE TO MY FACE IN THE DRAWINGS OF MYSELF

BEFORE NOW

FROM NOW ON

(THIS WILL BE GOOD FOR ANOTHER 10 YEARS)

② I'VE FINALLY GIVEN UP ON MY LIFE-LONG DREAM OF BEING A TEEN HEART THROB

YUCK

GRODY

Lennie!

③ I'M ENDING MY WICKED WAYS OF WINE, WOMEN AND SONG

OKAY, OKAY... BEER, PLAYBOY AND M.T.V.

THE BiG PiCTURE

by Lennie "dEAdLine" Peterson

I've REALLY hAd ENOUGH

The Big Picture

by Lennie "Flash" Peterson

PRESENTING

Things that have been sent to me in the mail (ANONYMOUSLY no less...)

A PHOTO OF A BLUEBERRY PIE *

to Lennie

?

*it made me hungry

AN INSTRUCTION BOOK

I get the hint

HOW TO DRAW CARTOONS

A BEER

I thank you*

Bud Lite

*WHOEVER YOU ARE

A CAN OF "NINE LIVES PLUS" CHICKEN DINNER
(Ginger thanks you)

I smell "ENDORSEMENT"!

A COOL NECKLACE (although it PROBABLY makes me a member of some weird evil cult or something)

WELCOME, BROTHER... PRAISE BE TO FOO-FA

DOING this comic strip is very time consuming. It's easy to draw myself but drawing other characters is kind of a pain the neck

Jeez

Tick tick tick

So, from now on, I'll be taking a few short cuts that will make life easier for me drawing-wise

INK

Hopefully no one will notice

The Big Picture PRESENTS

HOW to IMPRESS the CHICKS!

Step 1: Tell them you're a cartoonist

Hi! I'm a cartoonist! Mind if I join you?

Step 2: Dazzle them with your all-consuming life long ambition

...And someday I'll be a suction cup doll!

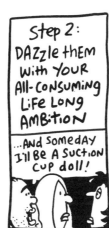

Step 3: Sit back and bask in their undivided love and admiration

Step 4: Try not to let all of the attention go to your head

Hey!! You'll see!!... "Heathcliff" did it!

There's a small hole in my bedroom floor where my radiator comes up. My cat sits there all day staring down into it.

Maybe there's a mouse down there. Or a bug... or she hears the cat that lives downstairs.

Or maybe it's a tattooed biker chick with a pierced tongue wearing a leather miniskirt and fishnet stockings.

I WAS WAITING TO BOARD the PLANE HOME FROM NEW YORK CITY

Dood!! I KNOW YOU!! You're IN that BAND! Hey! You're IN SEAT 25-B! Right Next to ME!!...DOOOD!

OH, MY GOD, Help me... This Flight is Sold Out... I'm Stuck with this GUY

BLAH BIAH ex-wife BIAH BLAH my HARLEY BIAH BLAH FIST Fight BIAH BIAH NAKED GIRLS BLAH BLAH

Jeez.. He's talking NON-STOP

It ONLY GOT WORSE

By the WAY, Dood, SORRY IF MY PITS KINDA STINK... I AIN'T SHOWERED SINCE MY FISHIN' TRIP LAST WEEK

AND NOW, IN RESPONSE TO YOUR CARDS, letters, FAXES, E-MAIL AND phone CALLS-

LAST WEEK'S STRIP EXPLAINED!!

Smelly, FAT, RED-NECKED, LOUD, OBNOXIOUS, WIFE-BEATING BIKER WHO HAS NO BUSINESS BEING ON the PLANet NEVERMIND AN AIRPLANE

ME

END

NOT FUNNY? BELIEVE ME, IT WASN'T FOR ME EITHER

This GUY "Ed" FROM ARIZONA WROTE to ME COMPLAINING that MY COMIC STRIP WASN'T FUNNY A FEW WEEKS AGO

Ed's CONFUSED. Ed thinks I GIVE A RAT's ASS WHAT Ed thinks

Ed PROBABLY LOOKS LIKE this

Ed should GET his OWN DAMN COMIC STRIP. He could CALL it "Ed the dork who's GOT WAY too much time ON his hands AND should LEAVE LENNIE PETERSON the Hell ALONE"

Ed's CONFUSED

The Big Picture

by Lennie "Got A Pen?" Peterson

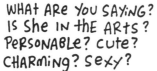

The Big Picture

BY Lennie "SHARPIE" PETERSON

I'VE BEEN thinking ABOUT something

uh oh

IN My comic STRIP, GINGER talks to HERSELF iN thought BALLOONS Like EVERY other dopey comic STRIP ANIMAL... I think I'M GONNA CHANGE that though

Huh?

I think I might use Just heR expressions FROM NOW ON...

the thought BALLOONS ARE too CONTRIVED

what do you think?

LENNIE, IF I told you once, I'VE told you A thousand times...

This is **Not** what your theRAPY sessions ARE FOR

PHD

ONE OF MY FAVORITE COMIC STRIPS IS "RHYMES WITH ORANGE" BY HILARY PRICE

HILARY HAS A FORMULA FOR CREATING YOUR VERY OWN SHOW BIZ NAME

① THINK OF YOUR CHILDHOOD PET'S NAME
② ADD YOUR MOTHER'S MAIDEN NAME ONTO THAT

THAT'S YOUR STAGE NAME! Cool, huh?

SEND YOURS to: THE Big Picture care of this NOOSE PAPER

(REAL) NAME

AND STREET

CITY   STATE/ZIP

STAGE NAME

CLIP 'N SEND!

WE'LL PUBLISH IT HERE PLUS YOU'LL RECEIVE THE REALLY SWELL GIFTS SHOWN BELOW!

WOW!

THANKS!! THIS IS SPARKY COLEMAN SAYING "MAKE IT A GREAT DAY!"

THAT'S IT... I'M CALLING HER VET

HELLO, DR. MANSFIELD? I THINK SOMETHING'S WRONG WITH MY CAT

REALLY? WHAT'S THE PROBLEM?

SHE'S BEEN AWAKE FOR MORE THAN TWENTY MINUTES

MUST BE NAP TIME

EVERY MOMENT OF OUR LIVES LEADS US TO EVERY PRESENT MOMENT

true

EVERY DECISION, LARGE AND SMALL, HAS PUT US IN THE PLACE WE'RE IN RIGHT HERE AND NOW

Cool, huh?

WHEN IT COMES RIGHT DOWN TO IT, YOU'VE LIVED YOUR ENTIRE LIFE JUST TO READ MY COMIC STRIP TODAY

Gee, thanks!

THE BIG PICTURE

by Lennie "dEAd-Line" Peterson

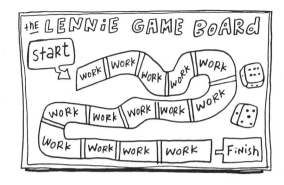

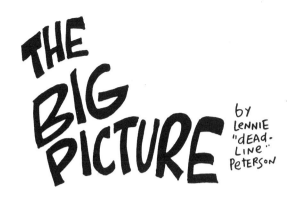

Hey Look! Wow! It's the Second Annual Big Picture Swim Suit Pin-up Poster!

Swim suit poster my Ass... there'd better be some "Fancy Feast" in this for me or I'm moving in with "Heathcliff"

For YOUR free copy of this poster, sneak into your dopey office at your dopey office job and photocopy the thing on your dopey copy machine! (You didn't think I was gonna send you one or something, did you? 'Cause I'm very busy.)

HEY!! Guess what?!! This comic strip is gonna be a BOOK!* Now the possibilities are ENDLESS!!

*I got a book contract! Whoa!

Ginger's Special edition "Big Picture" Gourmet Fancy Feast Cat Food

Picture dark roast coffee beans! (Mountain grown!)

"Big Picture" Lifesize Lennie Blow-Up Love doll! (it talks!) HEY BABY (For women only... sorry fellas!)

Big Picture sheets and pillow cases!

Big Picture beer!

First it might help if you would actually start working on the BOOK

ANDREWS McMEEL EDITOR

that's a detail... HEY!! HOW 'BOUT "THE BIG PICTURE" special edition custom Mercedes SLK"!!

Now I actually have to get ORGANIZED so I can put my BOOK together

I've got two C.d. covers to finish, six illustrations for a local newsletter...

...I work three nights a week with the band, I've got TONS of free-lance work, a "fine art" commission AND I have THREE girlfriends

Call me crazy but it just doesn't get any better than this!

you're talking to your cat

I JUST WANT to THANK YOU... FiNALLY, MY COMic STRiP got NoTicED... AND AFTER ALL is SAiD AND DoNE **YOU** WERE the ONLY ONE who Stood BY ME UNCONDitioNALLY... Even in the **WORST** of times **YOU** WERE ALWAYS THERE FOR ME PUSHING ME to SUCCEED! LifTiNG ME to the Highest HEiGHTs WHile EVERYONE Else LOST FAiTH! THERE WERE REALLY Rough times RECENTLY But WE PULLED Through it **TOGETHER**!!

SNIFF

YOU REALLY FiND OUT who YOUR FRIENDS ARE

JENN, IT's LENNIE... ONE OF MY NEWS-PAPERS SUGGESTED I HAVE A STEADY GiRLFRiEND AS A COUNTERPART TO MY CHARAC-TER iN MY COMiC STRiP!... INTEREST-ed??

CAN'T YOU JUST **INVENT** A STEADY GiRLFRiEND?

Jeez... THAT SOUNDS Like ACTUAL **WORK**

C'MON... MY STRiP is About MY REAL LiFE... JUST BE MY STEADY GiRLFRiEND FOR AWHile, OKAY? WE'LL HAVE LOTS OF WACKY AdVENTURES together ANd I'll WRiTE About 'EM

YOU'D HAVE to **KidNAP** ME to be **YOUR** STEADY GiRL-FRiEND

GREAt! -THAT'S A STARt!

I'M dOiNG WHAT I WAS BORN to do... I REALLY FEEL THAT WAY

I'M TRYiNG to MAKE the WORLD A Little BETTER PLACE to Live WiTH MY ARt AND MY MUSiC... IT's ALMOST LiKE I'M ON A MiSSiON FROM God!

THAT'S ALL REALLY WONDERFUL, MR. PETERSON

But YOU STiLL nAve to PAY YOUR TAXES

dAMN

THE BIG PICTURE

by LENNIE "don't try this at home" PETERSON

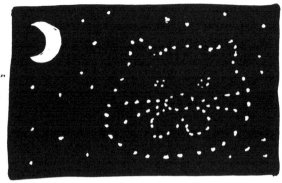

MY FIRST MEETING with MY BOOK PUBLISHER· NO doubt they'll BE dAZZLed BY MY SHREWD Negotiating Skills

OKAY, I HEAR JIM DAVIS makes Like FiFteeN MillioN dollARs A yEAR ON those "GARField" BOOKS

BUT **ME**, SiNCE I'M iN A good mood todAY...

...**I'VE** decided to stARt out With YOU FOR A MERE **TEN** MillioN the FiRSt yEAR

Heh Heh

HA HA HA HA HA HA Hee Hee HEE HA HA HO HO HA HA HO HO HA AHO H HF H
At LEAST they Still think YOU'RE FUNNY

MY EDITOR TOLD ME I COULD GET A LOT OF NEW READERS FOR MY COMIC STRIP IF I'D MAKE A REFERENCE TO **STAR TREK** ONCE IN AWHILE

A FRIEND OF MINE SAYS THAT MENTIONING THE **GRATEFUL DEAD** NOW AND THEN WOULD DO THE TRICK 'CAUSE DEAD FANS ARE **FANATICAL**

BUT I TOLD THEM BOTH, IN NO UNCERTAIN TERMS, "NO THANKS, MY COMIC STRIP CAN STAND ON IT'S **OWN** MERIT"

JEEZ, WHAT DO THEY TAKE ME FOR, A **SELLOUT**?

WHAT DO YOU SUPPOSE SHE'S THINKING ABOUT?

I DUNNO, JACKIE... CATS SEEM SO DEEP

SO STILL AND FOCUSED ... VERY MEDITATIVE

I GUESS WE'LL NEVER KNOW THE DEPTHS OF AN ANIMAL'S MIND SET

BUG

I'D LIKE TO THANK MY FRIEND NORMAN FOR ALL OF HIS SUPPORT

WOW! THAT'S GREAT! A BOOK DEAL! CONGRATULATIONS!

NORMAN

YOU KNOW, I'VE BEEN BEHIND YOU ALL THE WAY! I **KNEW** YOU COULD DO IT!

Gee, THANKS NORMAN

I THINK "YOU SHOULDA NEVER QUIT BERKLEE", "YOU'LL NEVER MAKE IT" AND "YOUR CARTOONS SUCK" WERE PROBABLY THE MOST ENCOURAGING

FOR VARIOUS REASONS I'm thinking OF CHANGING the NAME OF this Comic Strip to "DAILY DIARY"

Why?

Well, it truly IS ABOUT MY LiFE ON A dAiLY BASiS AND I think People Like that

WiLL it BE the SAME thing with A different NAME?

Oh, YA... SAME thing

SO it Still WON'T BE FUNNY?

I've started oil PAiNTiNG. It's ALL I think ABout NOW. It's ALL I do.

My FRIENDS AND FAMILY SAY it's AFFecting My relationships

BABy, it's three A.M. come to bed NOW

I'm kind of busy HERE

My Book publisher AND My SyNdicate both ARE concerned ~~the~~ that ALL OF My time Spent ON My "FiNe ART" will HAVE A NEGATiVE AFFect ON the QuALity of WoRK iN My comic strip

I told them there's ~~this~~ Nothing to WORRy ABout

ME *

* With A BEARD (old pHoto)

CARTOON ME

IT SEEMS LiKE tHERE's two Kinds OF PEOPLE iN the WORLD

Huh?

Theres the people who tell ME they think My drAWings of MyseLf look EXACTLY Like ME AND tHERE's the People who tell ME My drAWings look Nothing Like ME

AND Just think...

Neither IS A ComPLiMENt

The Big Picture

Written by Lennie Peterson, pencils by Lennie Peterson, inked by Lennie Peterson, layouts by Lennie Peterson, lettering by Lennie Peterson, photocopies and running around like a madman by Lennie Peterson, promotion and marketing by Lennie Peterson, sacrifices, suffering, starving and tortured artist syndrome by Lennie Peterson. Lennie Peterson's wardrobe provided by Todd Rawley and "Handmedowns Inc." Typing and "Sharpies" provided by Todd's mother. Borrowed and begged monies and moral support provided by her sister. Work ethic provided by her father. Inspiration provided by overdue credit card bills.

The people that will buy my book are **PIONEERS.** Patrik

these people will change the **FACE** of the comics pages by supporting my comic strip!

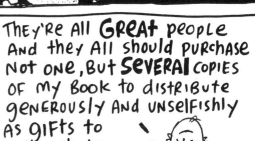

Men and women on the cutting edge! Pushing comic strips to the limit - **SWEEPING** out the old and ushering in the new!

They're all **GREAT** people and they all should purchase not one, but **SEVERAL** copies of my book to distribute generously and unselfishly as gifts to **all** of their loved ones!

then my comic strip will appear in newspapers all over the world thanks to those wonderful people who bought **SEVERAL** copies of my book!

You're gonna put **this** in your book, aren't you

So what are you saying?

Recently I've had an incredible period of spiritual growth. I've felt it coming off and on for **YEARS** now

I meditate at least twice a day...

I read, I study, and I think about all things spiritual

But, still, there's one thing that brings me closer to my "Higher Self" than anything else

Medium... regular, one sugar

My deadline to get this comic strip done for the week was yesterday

But I had to go to New York yesterday

I was hoping something funny would happen there for the sake of the comic strip and you, my faithful reader

But to be perfectly honest, nothing really funny happened

DAMN

SORRY

My niece, Jackie, thinks my cat is funny looking

Just ask... What's the harm in asking?..

'Cause... that's stoopid

But it's **crooked**... I don't see the harm in asking

First of all, it's just fine

And second

Vets don't **do** nose jobs

Are you sure? I don't see the harm in asking

You worked about 85 hours this week

Yep... EVERY week, mom

You know those FISH that struggle and struggle to get upstream only to DIE of exhaustion when they finally get to where they wanted to go?

I like a man who listens to his mother

It takes me about two hours to create this comic strip from start to finish EVERY week

PICASSO

It takes the average reader about 20 seconds to READ my comic strip

I don't get it

The way I see it, you each owe me about one hour, 59 minutes and 40 seconds-

I'll call you... ALL of you

Hello, Annie Aaronson from Arizona?... My name is Lennie and you probably read my comic strip in the newspaper down there and you owe me about... Hello?... Hello?..

PHONE BOOK

I went to visit my sister Melinda

My girl-friend says I'm moody

Do YOU think I'm moody?

ROBB REPORT

Which personality?

ROBB REPORT

THE BIG PICTURE

by Lennie

"INSUFFICIENT FUNDS"

Peterson

I'VE done A Lot OF SOUL SearchiNg these PaST Few YEARS... ReAdiNg, thiNking, meditAtiNg, LearNiNg... SeekiNg the TRUth ABout LiFe ANd why we're HERE

ANd deSpite what SOME OF US Believe...

..the ANSWER is NO+ LAyiNg AROuNd ALL dAy GROOMiNG oNeSelF while SoMEONE NAMEd LENNIE CATERS to OUR EVERY WHIM!!

I beg to differ

ANd So does YOUR GIRL-FRIEND

MY FRieNd's SeVeN YEAR OLd dAughter EMILY GAVE ME A BiRthdAy PReSeNt

Gee, EMILY, thANks... "the SPice GiRLs A to Z PHOTOGRAPHic ReFeReNce Book VoLUME FOUR"... JUST whAT I'Ve ALwAys wANTed —

CAN I BORROW it?

I'Ve discoveRed SoMethiNg that SeEMS to SolVe the PuZZLe OF ALL ReligioNs, FAiths ANd SPiRitUAL MYSteRies

THERE SeeMS to Be A UNiVeRsAL LAW OF "AttRActioN" wheRE EVERYONE ANd EVERYthiNg ReceiVES whATeVER it FocuSes ON OR ExPects

Both "Good" OR "BAd"; we get the BALANce OF whATeVER OUR thoughts ARE... FocuS ON LACK OF MONEY, we get LACk OF MONEY... ExPect HeALth, You Get HeALth

whAT do You thiNk?

Looks Like You "ExPected" to BORE YOUR GIRLFRIeNd to SLeEP with YOUR PHiLoSoPHicAL RAMBLiNgs there, oh MYSticAL CARTOON BOY

JENN?

ON THE ROAD AGAIN...

...And they've got A FREE CONTINENTAL BREAKFAST And COFFEE IN THE HOTEL LOBBY SO I JUST BROUGHT All My WORK STUFF DOWN **HERE**...Good idEA, huh? **VERY** CONVENIENT!

I'M LEAVING FOR MY CONCERT

Jeez, YOU'RE **REALly** PREOCCUPIED With YOUR Comic StRip

PREOCCUPIED?

YA... It's **ALL** YOU think ABOUT!

WHAT MAKES YOU SAY **thAt**?

HAVE A NICE CONCERT

And IN this SECTION OF THE GALLERY ARE LENNIES ORIGINAl Comic StRips

They'RE PRICED At About ONE HUNDRED DOLLARS And NO doubt they'll INCREASE IN VALUE WHEN his BOOK IS PUBLISHED

Hmmm

does HE HAVE ANY **FUNNY** ONES?

THE BIG PICTURE

by Lennie
"Mil-Lennie-um"
Peterson

This is incredible...it says here that most computer systems aren't "Y2K" compliant

It says that when the years shift from '99 to '00, a major state of **CHAOS** will occur

Computer systems, satellites, airlines, health care, electricity, manufacturing, telephones... All will **FAIL!**

Do you know what this **MEANS?**

NO CABLE T.V.!

And no **PIZZA DELIVERIES!!**

Quick! Grab your checkbook! I'll go to Blockbuster and Papa Gino's to stock up!

Did you see "Titanic"?

Ya... I thought it was stoopid

NOW ON VIDEO!

WHAT? HOW CAN YOU SAY that?.. I CRied Like A BABY through that whole movie... it WAS SO REAL

God, you men Are so IN-SEN-Sitive

...AND IN the NEWS tonight, the STAND-OFF CONTINUES At A GRADE School IN OKLAHOMA WHERE two ARMED GUNMEN ARE holding A CLASSROOM OF CHILDREN HOSTAGE

WANT SOME chips?

Well, JIM, I JUST LOVE to dRAW

Gotta HAND it to HIM

WART RADIO

I simply do it 'CAUSE I CAN't Help it!

the MAN's got A PASSION

Why, I'd do it FOR FREE!

FOR Lying

POSSIBLE BOOK titLES

FOR my Big time Book dEAL

1. "Hey, CHECK it Out! I got A Big time BOOK dEAL!"

2. "GARFIELD who?"

3. "WORCESTER ON Five dollARS A dAY"

4. "SPARKY COLEMAN- the myth, the MAN"

5. "dAGWOOD, ShmAGWOOD"

6. "IF YOU'RE A BALD, Big LIPPED, FORtiesh, divORCED, CAt OWNING SEx-CRAZED, VEGETARIAN ARtiSt/tROmBONiSt/ CARtOONISt/ex-tEACHER FROm CENtRAL MASSA- CHUSEttS this BOOK IS FOR YOU!"

7. "my CAt's BEttER thAN YOUR CAt"

8. "All LENNiE All the tiME!"

9. "All those OtHER BOOKS SUCK... BUY MINE."

10. "diLBERT ShmILBERT"

11. "WHOA! A BOOK dEAL! tAttOOEd BIKER CHICKS with PIERCED tONGUES WEARING LEATHER MINISKIRTS AND FIShNEt StOCKINGS will LOVE this!"

12. "How COME those 'FAMILY CIRCUS KIDS NEVER get old?"

13. "GINGER the COFFEE CRAZED CAt"

14. "HEY, NORMAN...Bite ME."

FINISHED... See you in the funny papers...